GALLERIA

26 Shopping Centers in Europe

GALLERIA
26 Shopping Centers in Europe

Edited by Shoichi Muto

First published in 1994 by
Graphic-sha Publishing Co., Ltd.©
1-9-12, Kudan-kita, Chiyoda-ku, Tokyo 102 Japan
Phone: 81-3-3263-4318
Fax: 81-3-3263-5297

Printed in Singapore by Toppan Printing Co., (Singapore) PTE., Ltd.
ISBN4-7661-0792-6 C2052

GALLERIA

ガレリア

ヨーロッパのショッピングセンター　26

Contents

目 次

FOREWORD

Even in Europe where people take pride in the appearance of cities and sensitively respond to its changes, significant changes have been seen in the construction and development of commercial facilities, office buildings, residences, etc. during the last quarter of a century. After the 1970s, when improved productivity due to industrialization had caused growth in personal consumption and ushered in the age of the automobile, residential areas expanded towards the periphery of cities, where suburban hypermarkets and large commercial facilities were developed. These facilities have brought about drastic changes in people's lives and consumption styles. Meanwhile, many facilities and arcades, which form the core of urban commercial areas, were constructed between the end of the last century and the beginning of this century, and in view of the obsolescence of these structures, renovation projects for their rejuvenation were implemented from 1980 to 1990. In the 1990s, the worldwide economic slump has created a wiser society, and those projects have been realized, although there might have been a delay or modification some of them.

Shopping centers are said to have their starting point in arcades. The oldest arcade in Europe is "The St. Hubertus Galleries" whose construction was completed in 1847 in Brussels. It is well known, along with the "Galleria Vittorio Emanuele II" in Milano, which also dates from the same period. Both feature a dome in the center.

More than a century has passed since the appearance of those old arcades, and although there have been changes such as the increased size and the number of tenants, present-day shopping centers remain unchanged in that an all season gallery (galleria) type, mall style facility with an atrium is the mainstream design. Major differences lie in the change of structural lines from horizontal, plain ones to vertical, solid ones due to the adoption of a multi-level structure, which requires the dynamic arrangement of approaches, staircases, elevators, escalators and other means of transportation.

はじめに

都市の風貌に誇りを抱き その変貌には敏感に反応を示すヨーロッパにおいても この四半世紀の間に 商業施設やオフィスビル 住宅などの建設 開発面で大きな変化が見られた。工業化による生産性の向上が より個人消費の伸びを呼び 車時代を迎えた1970年代以降には 住宅地域は都市周辺へと拡大し 郊外型のハイパーマーケットや大型商業施設が開発され 生活や消費スタイルを変革させた。一方 都市における商業地域の中心である施設やアーケードは 前世紀末から今世紀初頭に建設された例が多く その老朽化にともない 活性化を図った再開発プロジェクトが1980年から1990年にかけて具体化をみるに至った。90年代に入り 世界的に陥った経済不況が いい意味での成熟した社会の到来を招き プロジェクトは 一部に遅れや見直しなどの影響があったであろうものの 実現され現在に至っている。

ショッピングセンターの原点はアーケードにあるといわれる。ヨーロッパで最古のアーケードとしては 1847年に完成したブリュッセルの〈セント フバルタス=The St.Hubertus Galleries〉や ミラノの〈エマニエーレ 2世アーケード=Galleria Vittorio Emanuele II〉がよく知られるところで いずれも中央にドームを持っている。
それから1世紀以上をへて 建設される現在のショッピングセンターは 規模やテナント数の増などの変化はあるものの 全天候型でアトリウムを持つ ギャラリー形式(ガレリア=Galleria)のモールがデザインの主流であることは変わっていない。大きな違いとしては 動線が水平で平面的なものから多層にわたる構造の変化により 立体的で垂直な動きが加わったことで その移送の手段として アプローチや階段 エレベーター エスカレーターなどに工夫がこらされている。

It is no exaggeration to say that the only requirement for making a shopping center operation a success, is the capability to attract shoppers. In other words, it is vital to make the facility attractive enough to be repeatedly utilized by customers, that is, the key to success lies in securing as many repeater customers as possible. For this purpose, it is absolutely necessary to create a comfortable space which can be utilized without being affected by weather or temperature. Designing such a space is an important task that architects and designers are required to do, along with securing attractive tenants, allotting space, holding various events, and other requirements for facility operation.

In the course of the current data collecting trip, I saw that shopping centers are changing in nature from a mere composite commercial facility to a more public facility, planned in the image of a near futuristic plaza in front of a city hall, and that they are constructed together with various other facilities (e.g. multi-function facility, amusement facility, hotel, office, residential quarter), so that they can perform town-, community- or even small city-wide functions. Also, contrary to my expectations, the majority of visually exciting designs were created from traditional and composed architectural designs. Are these expressions of "continuity of space" and "timelessness of structure" which lie at the basis of ideas of the European architects, etc.?

This book details 26 shopping centers (including one under construction) whose construction was completed between 1991 and 1993 in 23 cities in 10 European countries.

At "ZEILGALERIE LES FACETTES" in Frankfurt, Germany, a unique idea was adopted: guests are guided by escalators up to the highest floor, and then allowed to walk down clockwise to the 1st floor along a gently sloped aisle. At "MONUMENT MALL" in Newcastle, U.K., a historical space is reproduced in the mall, and high tech sense is also stressed by uniformly distributing natural light from the atrium to all floors. At the "MÉTROPOLE CENTRE," situated in La Chaux-de-

---

　成功するショッピングセンターの条件としてはその集客性がすべてと言っても過言ではない。魅力ある施設として 客に繰り返し利用してもらうこと つまり いかにリピーターを確保するかである。天候や気温に左右されずに利用できる快適空間づくりが絶対条件である。吸引力のあるテナントの確保とそのミックス 各種イベントなどとともに そのためのデザイニングが 建築家 デザイナーに要求される重要なポイントである。

　今回 取材にあたって感じたことは ショッピングセンターが 単なる複合商業施設としてでなく より公共性をもたせた近未来の"市庁舎前広場"的なイメージで計画され 多目的施設 アミューズメント施設 ホテル オフィス 住宅などの併設や 街 地域ぐるみ あるいは小都市の機能を持たせた施設づくりへと変わってきていることであった。

　また 視覚的にエキサイティングなデザイニングとは 意外にも 伝統的で落ち着いた建築デザインが 大半を占めたことであった。それは ヨーロッパのクリエイターの 発想の根底にある "空間の継続性" であり "造形物の不偏性(timeless)" の現れなのでであろうか。

　本書にはヨーロッパの10ケ国 23の都市に 1991年から93年までに完成した26店(1店は建設中)のショッピングセンターを取材し収録している。

　取材店でみると ドイツ・フランクフルトの〈ツァイルガレリー レ ファセット＝ZEILGALERIE LES FACETTES〉では 客を最上階までエスカレーターで誘導し 1階までゆるいスロープの通路を設け 時計回りに回遊させるという発想がユニークである。イギリス・ニューカッスルの〈モニュメント モール＝MONUMENT MALL〉では モールに歴史的空間を再現し

Fonds, Switzerland, which is near the French border, the atrium space is crossed by a bridge joining the selling areas, and because the sides of the bridge are finished with arched mirrors, in which the interior scenes are reflected, visual expanse is given to the interior space. At "THE BENTALL CENTRE," in Kingstone, U.K., which has the largest atrium among the shopping centers covered in the current collection, escalators are inclined against the selling space so that shoppers can have a wide-angled view of the mall interior. At "HEUVEL GALERIE," in Eindhoven, Netherlands, staircases are effectively placed under the dome so that the interior space as a whole is designed to look like a theater where many events are held. Thus, the facility has succeeded in gaining popularity. "THOMAS NEAL'S," in Covent Garden, London, preserves the architectural structure and designs of the Victorian age by presenting them in a patio style, thus transmitting the history. Meanwhile, in accordance with the opening of French national railways' T.G.V., "EURALILLE," in Lille, France, is presented as a space for the 21st century, which is composed of facilities now under construction.

I would be pleased if readers refer to this book not only for shopping center designing, but also for finding hints on comfortable space making concepts or creative approaches.

In closing, I would like to express my heart-felt thanks to the shopping centers, architects and designers who cooperated in data collection and photography, and also to Mr. Hiroshi Tsujita, Graphic-sha Publishing Co., Ltd., for editing, Mr. Minoru Morita for layout, and to all of the other people concerned.

September 1994
Shoichi Muto
In the suburbs of Stockholm

ハイテク感覚を強調し アトリウムからの自然光が各フロアに万遍なくまわるよう工夫されている。スイスのフランス国境に近い ラ ショー デュ フォンの〈メトロポール センター＝MÉTROPOLE CENTRE〉では アトリウムの空間をブリッジで横切り 売り場をジョイントしているが 側面をアーチ状のミラー張りにすることで 写り込みを利用し視覚的に広がりを持たせている。今回の取材の中で 最大規模のアトリウムを有する イギリス・キングストーンの〈ザ ベンタル センター＝THE BENTALL CENTRE〉では売り場に対して エスカレーターを斜めに設置することで モール内を広角的に見せる工夫をしている。オランダ・アイントホーフェンの〈ホイフェル ガレリー＝HEUVEL GALERIE〉では ドームの下に階段を効果的に設置し 劇場のようなデザイニングで 多くのイベントをマルチで催し人気を博している。ロンドンのコベントガーデンの〈トーマス ニールス＝THOMAS NEAL'S〉は ヴィクトリア時代の建築構造とデザインを残し パティオ調にまとめ 歴史を今に伝えている。フランス・リールの〈ユーラリール＝EURALILLE〉は フランス国鉄 TGVの開通に合わせ 21世紀を意識した空間構成の施設を建設中である。

本書から単に ショッピングセンターのデザインのみでなく 快適な空間づくりのコンセプトや創作のためのヒントを読みとっていただければ幸いである。

最後に 取材 撮影にあたって ご協力いただいたショッピングセンター及び 建築家 デザイナー各位 編集にあたっては グラフィック社の辻田 博氏 レイアウトの森田 実氏 ほか 関係各位に厚く感謝いたします。

1994年 9 月／ストックホルム近郊にて

武藤聖一

THE BENTALL CENTRE

〈Kingstone, UK〉

Having a long history (founded in 1867), Bentalls has continued to grow along with the community. In November 1992, it opened "THE BENTALL CENTRE" centering around "Bentalls" (department store), as part of an urban land redevelopment project. This shopping center is the largest facility in the U.K. — a 4-storied building with 42,734 m² of total selling space and an arched atrium 31 m high and 150 long. The glazed ceiling of the atrium is covered with #-shaped aluminum frames (made by Space Deck, U.K.) whose joints are decorated with about 2,000 lights (through fibre optics) — the largest feature of the facility.

In order to give attractive and wide-angled views to the mall, the features of the atrium are fully utilized by means of escalators inclined against the selling area, ramps instead of staircases, and others. On the highest floor there are a cafe, a restaurant and also a takeout shop composed of 5 units, and in the atrium, which introduces natural light from boat-shaped ceiling, a 400-seat food court is located to offer a comfortable space.

キングストーンの Bentalls 社は 1867年創立という歴史を持ち 地域の発展とともに歩み続ける会社であるが 市街地再開発により〈Bentalls〉(百貨店)を核にしたこの 〈ザ ベンタル センター＝THE BENTALL CENTRE〉を1992年11月にオープンさせた。4層の建物でアーチ型の高さ31メートル 長さ150メートルのアトリウムを持つこのショッピングセンターは総売場面積 42,734㎡で 英国最大の規模である。アトリウムの ガラス天井は ♯状のアルミフレーム(英国・Space Deck社製)で覆われ そのジョイント部分には約2,000個のライト(ファイバー オプティック ライト＝fibre optic light)が取り付けられ 施設最大のポイントとなっている。また エスカレーターを 売り場に対し斜めに設置したり 空間に階段室を設けずタラップ状の階段を設置するなど アトリウムの持つ特長をフルに活かし 立体的に 広角的にモールを見せる(感じさせる)工夫がなされている。最上階には 5ユニットで構成されたカフェ レストランテイクアウトショップがあり ボート形の天井から 自然光を採り入れたアトリウムには 400席のフードコートが設けられ 快適な空間を構成している。

● THE BENTALL CENTRE

Address:	Clarence Street Kingstone Upon Thames Surrey, UK
Opened:	November 2, 1992
Developer:	Norwich Union, Bentalls plc.
Design:	Building Design Partnership, Space Decks Ltd.
Area:	42,734 m²
Number of cars parked:	1,200
Key tenants:	Bentalls, W. H. Smith, Dillons
Number of tenants:	100

●ザ ベンタル センター

住所：	Clarence Street Kingstone Upon Thames Surrey, UK
開店：	1992年11月2日
デベロッパー：	Norwich Union, Bentalls plc.
設計：	Building Design Partnership, Space Decks Ltd.
面積：	42,734㎡
駐車台数：	1,200
キーテナント：	Bentalls, W H Smith, Dillons
テナント数：	100

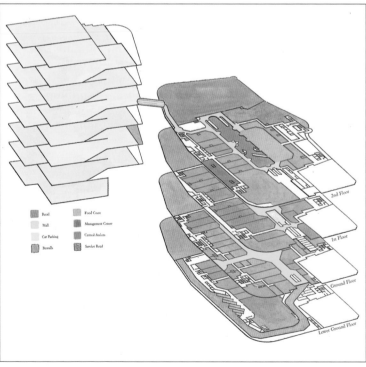

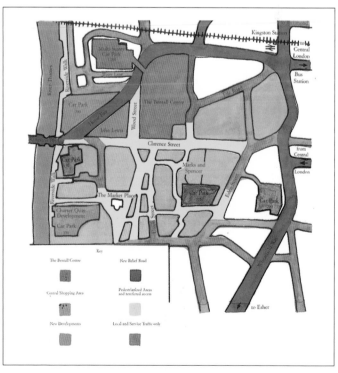

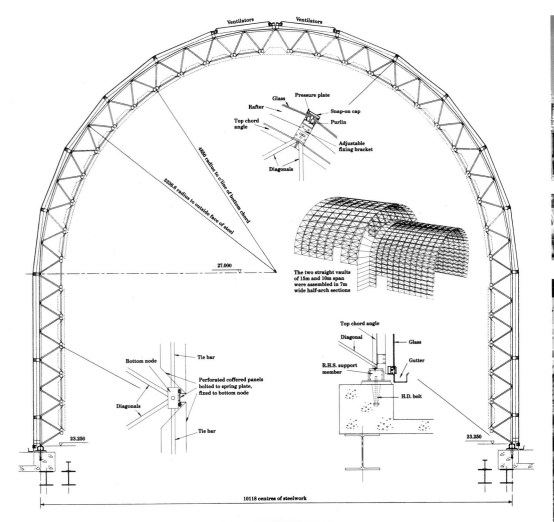

Ventilators Ventilators

Pressure plate

Glass

Rafter Snap-on cap

Top chord angle Purlin

Adjustable fixing bracket

Diagonals

4860 radius to c/line of bottom chord

5356.6 radius to outside face of steel

27.000

The two straight vaults of 15m and 10m span were assembled in 7m wide half-arch sections

Top chord angle

Diagonal

Glass

R.H.S. support member

Gutter

H.D. bolt

Bottom node

Tie bar

Perforated coffered panels bolted to spring plate, fixed to bottom node

Diagonals

Tie bar

23.250

23.250

10118 centres of steelwork

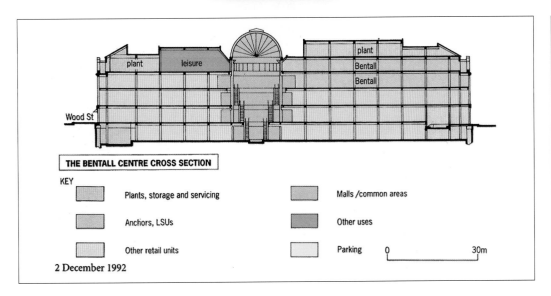

The Bentall Centre cross section.

plant leisure

plant

Bentall

Bentall

Wood St

THE BENTALL CENTRE CROSS SECTION

KEY

Plants, storage and servicing

Anchors, LSUs

Other retail units

Malls /common areas

Other uses

Parking

0   30m

2 December 1992

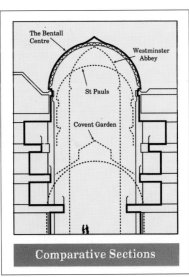

The Bentall Centre

Westminster Abbey

St Pauls

Covent Garden

Comparative Sections

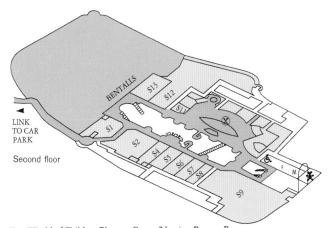

Second floor

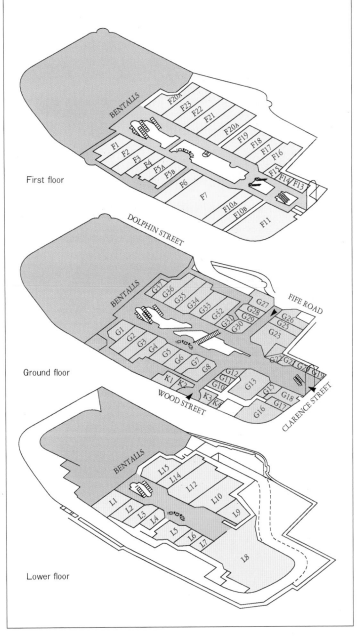

First floor

Ground floor

Lower floor

15

SÖDERHALLARNA

〈Stockholm, Sweden〉

In recent years, the area extending from the national railway's Södrastin Station in Södermalm, an island on the southern side of Stockholm, to the subway system's Medborgerplatsen has undergone a lot of redevelopment and renewal, and is currently very brisk as an area for young people. Opened in the fall of 1992, "SÖDERHALLARNA" is a composite building having a total area of 30,100 m², and is tenanted by boutiques, restaurants, a movie theater, a market hall, offices, etc. The facility is composed of an office building and a commercial building called "Saluhall," which are separated by the central corridor.

The central part of the commercial building forms an atrium space supported by 8 red columns, and the ceiling, with a skylight, is 23 m high from the mosaicked floor. On the 1st floor, a food market in the traditional Swedish style has been reproduced, and from the balcony of the selling space on the upper floors, one can watch people walking through the space. The 2nd floor is composed of boutiques, the 1st basement, also of boutiques and a movie theater, and the 3rd to 5th floors, of restaurants.

The center of the office building forms an atrium 24 m high, and the cylindrical staircase leading to the ceiling and the pillars is painted green, giving an image of trees, and, from the ceiling, a sailboat is suspended to present the image of people enjoying boating, and a row of streets is also displayed. In the center of the 1st floor there is a ship-shaped bar counter. The basement is composed of a movie theater, the 1st and 2nd floors of boutiques, and the 3rd and higher floors of offices. The staircase leading to the 2nd floor is equipped with lighting and decorated with potted greenery, also serves as the food court of a takeout restaurant. Thus, this facility is drawing a lot of attention as the latest hot spot in Stockholm.

ストックホルムの南側の島 ゼーダーマルム（Södermalm）の 国鉄南駅（Södrastin）から地下鉄 Medborgerplatsen 駅に至る地区は 近年再開発やリニューアルが著しく 若者の街として活気のある場所である。〈ゼーダーハラーナ＝SÖDERHALLARNA〉は 地下に駐車場を持つブティックやレストラン 映画館 マーケットホール オフィスなどが入居したトータル 30,100㎡の複合ビルで 1992年秋にオープンした。この施設はオフィス棟と "Saluhall" と呼ぶ商業棟で構成し 中央のコリドールで分割されている。

商業棟の中心は 赤い 8本の円柱に支えられたアトリウムでモザイク模様の床から天窓のある天井までは23メートルの高さ。1階にはスウェーデンの伝統的なスタイルの食品マーケットが再現され 上層階の売り場のバルコニーからは人の流れが眺められる。2階がブティック 地下1階がブティックと映画館 3～5階がレストランの店舗構成になっている。

オフィス棟の中心は高さ24メートルのアトリウムで 壁面中央の天井へ続く 筒型の階段室と支柱は 樹木をイメージしグリーンでペイントされている。天井からは帆船がつり下げられ 船遊びをする人々と町並みを演出している。1階中央には船の形をしたバーカウンターがある。地階が映画館 1～2階 ブティック 3階以上はオフィスで構成。2階への階段は 照明とグリーンの植栽をセットして テイクアウトショップのフードコートも兼ねている。ストックホルムで最も新しいスポットとして話題になっている。

● SÖDERHALLARNA

Address:	Medborgarplatsen Stockholm, Sweden
Opened:	September 25, 1992
Developer:	Kungsfiskaren Bygg och Fastighet AB
Design:	Bo Kjessel Arkitektkontor AB
Area:	30,100 m²
Number of cars parked:	150

●ゼーダーハラーナ

住所：	Medborgarplatsen Stockholm, Sweden
開店：	1992年 9 月25日
デベロッパー：	Kungsfiskaren Bygg och Fastighet AB
設計：	Bo Kjessel Arkitektkontor AB
面積：	30,100㎡
駐車台数：	150
キーテナント：	Södermalms Saluhall
テナント数：	30

Key tenants:	Södermalms Saluhall
Number of tenants:	30

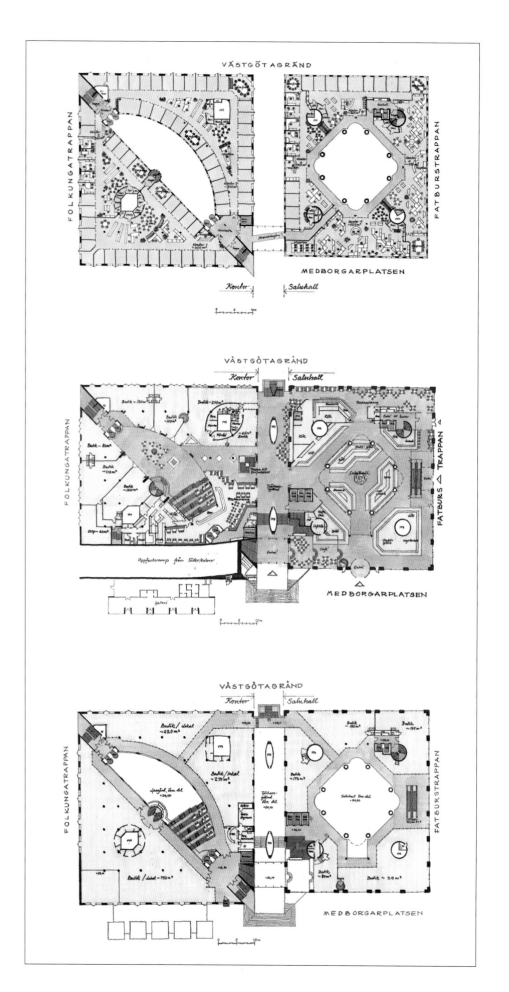

TRONDHEIM TORG

〈Trondheim, Norway〉

A shopping mall developed in the central area of Trondheim, the third city in Norway, situated to the north of Lat. 60°N. The facility mainly consists of 6 buildings which have been redeveloped. Due to differences in the owners, service conditions, height, etc. of those buildings, 4 years had to be spent in making adjustments with those concerned and municipal authorities from the start of project planning to the start of construction. However, construction was completed with exceptional speed — in only 8 months (from March 1992 when construction started to October of the same year when it was completed and the mall opened).

The layout of "TRONDHEIM TORG" is such that the 6 buildings are joined by a newly constructed mall at the Elephant Plassen (Plaza) in the center of the facility. There is also an arched glazed atrium with escalators, staircases, elevators, etc. Also by introducing natural light, the atrium space is dynamically designed. Since shops are placed around the atrium, the flow of shoppers is very smooth. The respective facades of tenant shops are uniquely designed so that the mall presents a varied but harmonious image. The parking lot, which is equipped with a lift system capable of accommodating 450 cars, is free of charge, and serving as an approach which can help increase guest capturing capability.

● TRONDHEIM TORG

Address: Kongensgt. 11 N-7011 Trondheim,
                        Norway
Opened: October 1992
Developer: Petter A. Stordalen, Agora Drift A/S
Design: Rødahl og Clausen A/S
Area: 12,000 m²
Number of cars parked: 450
Key tenants: Rema 1000, Hennes & Mauritz, Cubus,
                        Kappahl
Number of tenants: 35

北緯60度以北 ノルウェイの第三の都市トロンヘイム（Trondheim）の中心部に開発されたショッピングモール。既存の6棟のビルを中心に再開発されたもので 所有者や使用条件 建物の高さなどの違いから関係者や市当局との調整に プロジェクトが計画されてから着工までに 4年を費やしたという。しかし1992年 3月の工事着工から同年10月にオープンまで約8カ月という異例のスピードで完成された。この 〈トロンヘイム トリエ＝TRONDHEIM TORG〉は 施設の中央部 Elephant plassen（象の広場）に新しくモールを設け各建物をジョイントしている。ガラス張りでアーチ状のアトリウムを囲んだ店舗配置で 自然光を採り入れ 動きのあるデザインでまとめられ 人の流れが非常にスムーズである。リフトシステムを採用した駐車場（450台収容可能）が無料で開放され 集客力アップへのアプローチとなっている。

●トロンヘイム トリエ
住所：   Kongensgt. 11 N-7011 Trondheim, Norway
開店：   1992年10月
デベロッパー：Petter A. Stordalen, Agora Drift A/S
設計：   Rødahl og Clausen A/S
面積：   12,000㎡
駐車台数：   450
キーテナント：Rema 1000, Hennes & Mauritz, Cubus, Kappahl
テナント数：   35

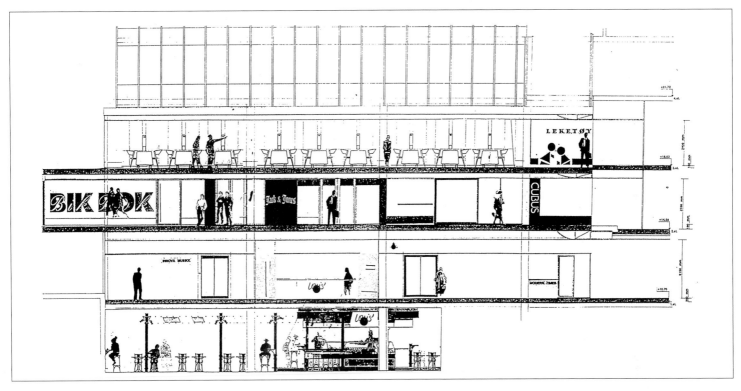

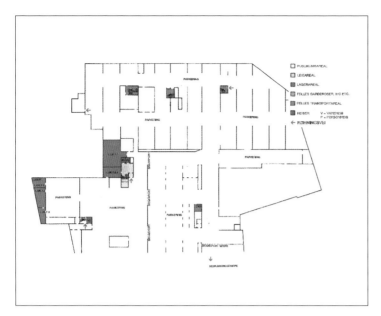

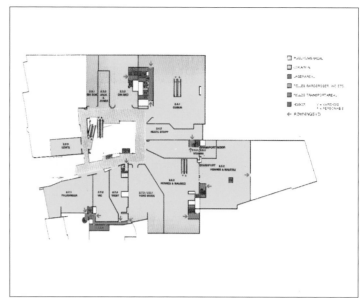

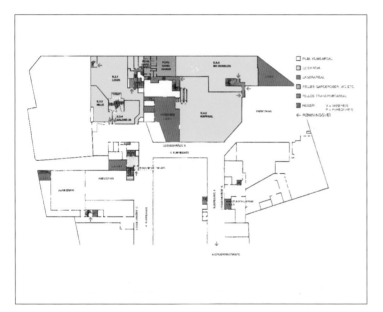

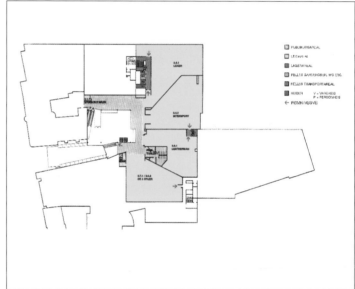

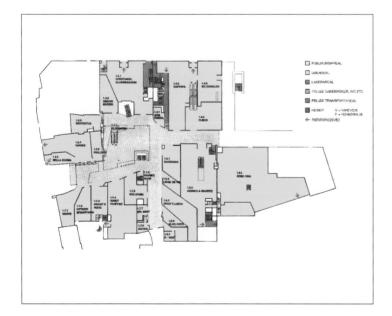

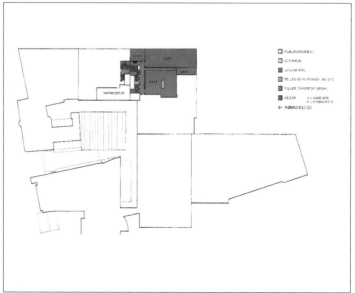

ZEILGALERIE LES FACETTES

〈Frankfurt, Germany〉

"ZEILGALERIE LES FACETTES" was created by demolishing a multi-purpose building on Zeil Street with a crowded vehicle-free promenade across a bustling street in Frankfurt, and constructing a new building adjoining the department store "Kaufhof." In the slender stairwell located in the center of the interior space, 6 escalators have been installed so that shoppers ride on them in sequence, and are thus conducted up to the multi-media center at Level 7 (8th floor). Since there are no escalators for descending, 2 elevators are utilized. Extending over about 500 m from the highest floor down to the 1st floor, there runs a gently sloped aisle which serves as an ideal promenade along which shoppers can enjoy window shopping at 70 shops. Shoppers descend in a clockwise direction while enjoying shopping — this innovative idea incorporated in the design is contributing a great deal to the capturing of customers. The floors from the basement up to the highest level look as if they are supported by red metallic pillars which rise upright, and a work of art by an Italian artist, Leonardo Mosso, which connects colored aluminum pins with rubber tubes, is extended in the space, thus enhancing the modern, artistic image of the interior space. This shopping center also stresses unique customer services, including child care in area called "Kinder Land" on the highest floor, and storage for coats, luggages, etc. in the basement cloakroom. At night, the facade is beautifully decorated with pickle lights. Even after closing, the highest floor is open as an observation deck so that it is always crowded with people and hotly talked about as an attractive spot in Frankfurt.

● ZEILGALERIE LES FACETTES
Address: Zeil 112-114 D-6000 Frankfurt, Germany
Opened: November 1992
Developer: Dr. Jürgen Schneider and Claudia Schneider-Granzow, Königstein im Taurus
Design: Professor Rüdiger Kramm + Aexl Strigl
Area: 22,000 m²
Key tenants: Marché Restaurant
Number of tenants: 60

フランクフルトの繁華街 並木道を挟んで歩行者天国でにぎわうZeil通りの 雑居ビルを壊し 百貨店〈Kaufhof〉と隣接させて再開発したのが〈ツァイルガレリー レ ファセット＝ZEILGALERIE LES FACETTES〉である。店内中央部の細く奥に長い吹抜け空間には 6基のエスカレーターが設置され 乗り継いでLevel 7（8階）のマルチメディアセンターへと誘導される。下り専用のエスカレーターは設置していないので 2基のエレベーターを利用するわけだが 最上階から 1階までの約500メートルはゆるやかなスロープがつけられた通路で 買い物や70店舗の ウインドショッピングが楽しめる絶好の散策路となっている。吹抜け空間に沿って 右から左へショッピングを楽しみながら 時計の回転方向に回遊しながら降りるという これまでにみられなかった新しい考えが設計に取り入れられ 集客につながる最大のポイントになっている。地階から最上階までの各階は 垂直に延びる赤いメタリックの柱に支えられているといった感じでイタリアのアーティスト レオナルド モッソー作のカラーアルミの棒（ピン）をゴム管でコネクトしたオブジェが空間に張られ 店内のモダンなアート感覚を高めている。このショッピングセンターではカスタムサービスにも力を入れ 最上階には "Kinder Land"と呼ぶスペースを設け子供を一時 預かったり 地階クロークでは コートや荷物を預かるなど他ではあまりみられない面での充実をはかっている。夜のファサードにはピクルスライトが流され美しい。最上階は閉店後も公開され 展望デッキとなっているため 常に人々が集まり フランクフルトのアトラクティブなスポットとして話題になっている。

● ツァイルガレリー レ ファセット
住所： Zeil 112-114 D-6000 Frankfurt, Germany
開店： 1992年11月
デベロッパー： Dr. Jürgen Schneider and Claudia Schneider-Granzow, Königstein im Taurus
設計： Professor Rüdiger Kramm + Aexl Strigl
面積： 22,000㎡
キーテナント： Marché Restaurant
テナント数： 60

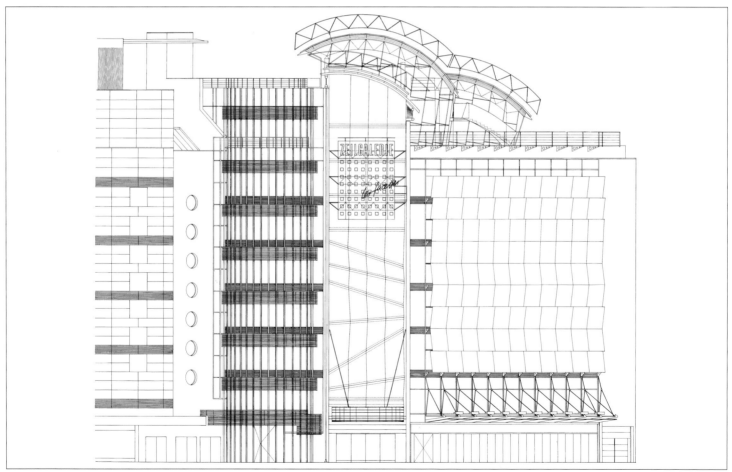

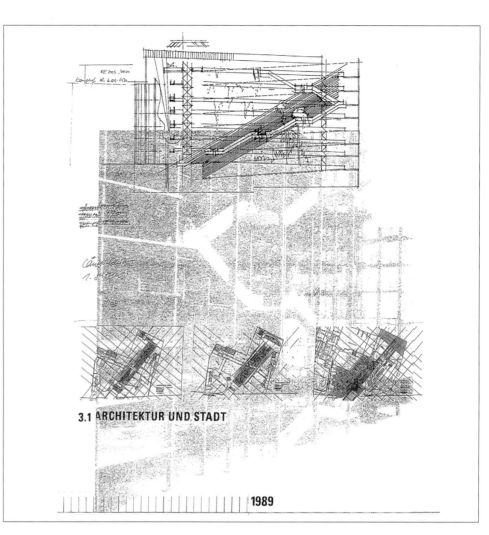

3.1 ARCHITEKTUR UND STADT

1989

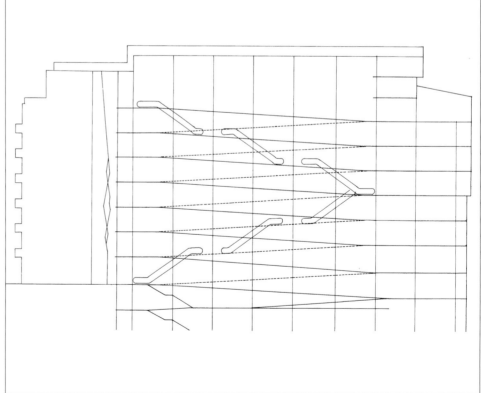

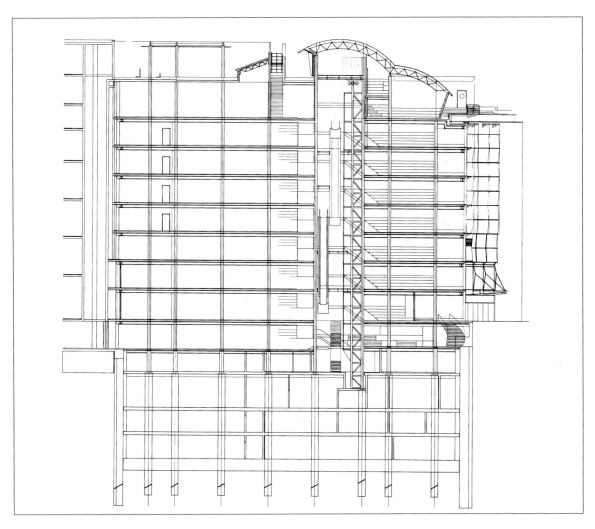

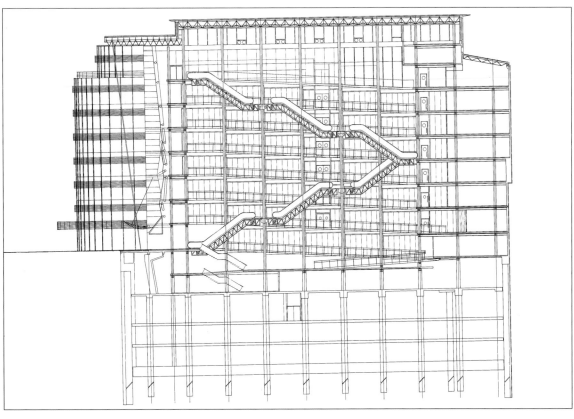

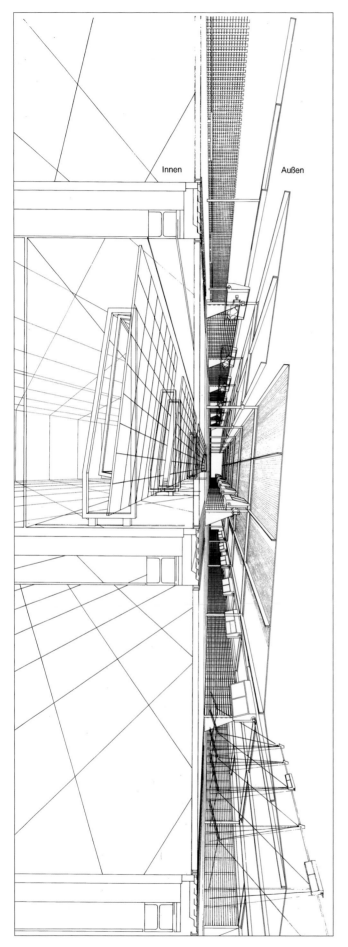

Innen   Außen

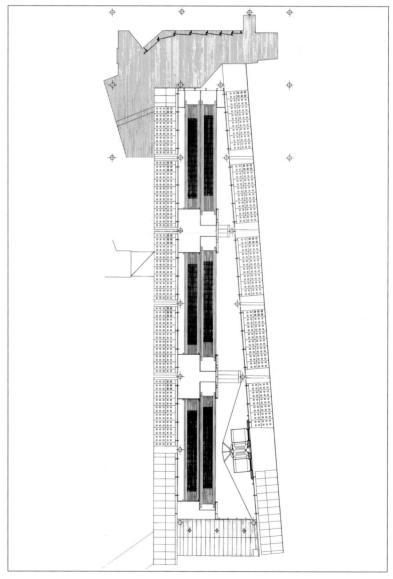

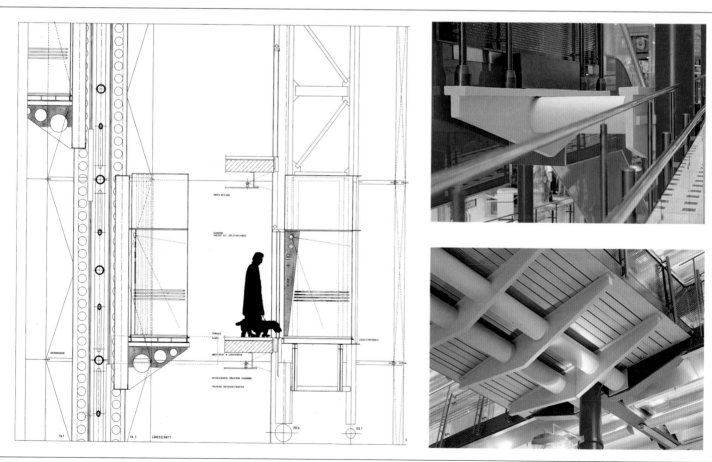

BARICENTRO

⟨Barberà del Vallés, Spain⟩

A suburban freestanding shopping center situated near Route 150 in the suburbs of Barcelona. The second phase of construction covering 42,600 m², has already been completed and this space is currently operating. Featuring a blue facade with columns installed by the entrance, the facility opened with a total space of 62,400 m², including 11 movie theaters and department store "C & A" sector. Tenanted by 150 shops centering around the do-it-yourself shop "AKI" and the hypermarket "Continente." The atrium is provided with joint stations leading to the respective floors, while escalators gently link the new and old centers. Shops operate on the right and left sides of a long two-level arcade. The central part of the mall is provided with benches for resting and a tower-like tank in which fish swim, presenting a refreshing environment to shoppers.

● BARICENTRO

Address: Carretera nacional 150 km 6,7
                     E-08210 Barberà del Vallés, Spain
Opened: July 1992
Developer: Promotora Catalana de desarrollo
                     Comercial S.A. Grupo Deico
Design: Horacio Dominguez
Area: 62,400 m²
Number of cars parked: 3,800
Key tenants: AKI, Continente, C & A
Number of tenants: 150

バルセロナの郊外 国道150号線沿いに位置する郊外型のショッピングセンター。既に営業中の42,600㎡の第2期工事分が完成 エントランスにコロン(柱)を配したブルーのファサードで 11の映画館と百貨店〈C & A〉部門を加えトータル 62,400㎡でオープンした。ドゥ イット ユアセルフの〈AKI〉と ハイパーマーケットの〈Continente〉を核テナントにし 150のテナントが出店している。アトリウムには各階へのジョイントステーションが設けられ エスカレーターがゆるやかに新旧のセンターをつないでいる。2層の長いアーケードの左右が店舗でモールの中央部分には休憩用のベンチや塔状の水槽が設けられ 魚が泳ぎ 利用客にさわやかな環境を提供している。

● バリセントロ

住所：   Carretera nacional 150 Km 6,7 E-08210 Barberà del
             Vallés, Spain
開店：   1992年7月
デベロッパー：Promotora Catalana de desarrollo Comercial S.A. Grupo
             Deico
設計：   Horacio Dominguez
面積：   62,400㎡
駐車台数：   3,800
キーテナント：AKI, Continente, C & A
テナント数：   150

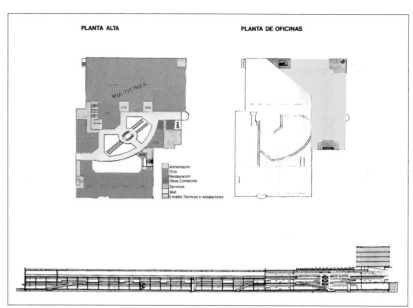

PLANTA ALTA

PLANTA DE OFICINAS

- Alimentación
- Ocio
- Restauración
- Otros Comercios
- Servicios
- Mall
- Locales Técnicos e Instalaciones

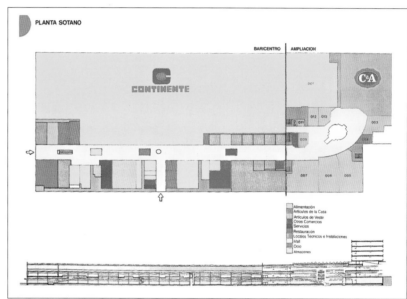

PLANTA SOTANO

BARICENTRO | AMPLIACION

CONTINENTE

C&A

- Alimentación
- Artículos de la Casa
- Artículos de Vestir
- Otros Comercios
- Servicios
- Restauración
- Locales Técnicos e Instalaciones
- Mall
- Ocio
- Almacenes

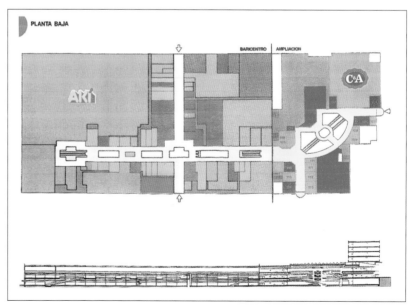

PLANTA BAJA

BARICENTRO | AMPLIACION

AKÍ

C&A

MÉTROPOLE CENTRE

〈La Chaux-de-Fonds, Switzerland〉

The "MÉTROPOLE CENTRE" is a shop complex developed by Migros (Société Coopérative Migros), a cooperative chain in Switzerland, and is situated in front of a station in La Chaux-de-Fonds, a town along the border with France, which lies behind the Jura when approached from Neuchâtel.

Within the fully glazed building there is an arched atrium in the central part which looks as if it divides the interior space in two. By introducing ample light, a bright, comfortable shop space has been created. The vast majority of tenants are shops belonging to the Migros group, including a supermarket in the basement, and textile and do-it-yourself shops. The parking space is located totally on underground so that 575 cars can be accommodated on 4 basement levels. The atrium is provided with 4 see-through elevators and a bridge across the 3 floors which, coupled with the interior escalators, link the selling corners. In order to give visual expanse to the interior space the sides of the bridge are finished with arched mirrors in which the interior scenes are reflected. There is also a cafe space on the bridge. Thus, because it is a place where shoppers can relax, the center is favorably accepted by customers.

● MÉTROPOLE CENTRE

Address:	Rue Daniel-Jeanrichard 29, 2300 La Chaux-de-Fonds, Switzerland
Opened:	March 30, 1993
Developer:	Migros Neuchâtel-Fribourg
Design:	Raphaël Brugger
Area:	44,000 m^2
Number of cars parked:	575
Key tenants:	Migros Neuchâtel-Fribourg
Number of tenants:	30

〈メトロポール センター＝MÉTROPOLE CENTRE〉は スイスのコーポチェーン Migros (＝Societe Coopérateve Migros) が開発したショップコンプレックスで ヌーシャテル (Neuchâtel) からジェラ (Jura) 山脈を越えた フランスとの国境沿いの町 La Chaux-de-Fonds の駅前に位置している。総ガラス張りの建物で 店内を2分するように中央部にアーチ形のアトリウムを設け充分な採光により 明るい快適な売り場構成をしている。テナントは 地階のスーパーマーケットをはじめ テキスタイル ドゥイット ユアセルフ など Migros系のショップが大半を占めている。駐車スペースはすべて地階にとり 4層で575台分を確保している。アトリウムには4基のシースルーエレベーターと 3フロアにわたってブリッジが架けられ 店内のエスカレーターとともに 各売り場を結んでいる。ブリッジの側面をアーチ状のミラー張りにすることで そこへの写り混みを利用し 視覚的に広がりをもたせている。 橋上にはカフェのスペースもあり 寛ぎの場として買い物客の人気を博している。

● メトロポール センター

住所：	Rue Daniel-Jeanrichard 29, 2300 La Chaux-de-Fonds, Switzerland
開店：	1993年3月30日
デベロッパー：	Migros Neuchâtel-Fribourg
設計：	Raphaël Brugger
面積：	44,000m²
駐車台数：	575
キーテナント：	Migros Neuchâtel-Fribourg
テナント数：	30

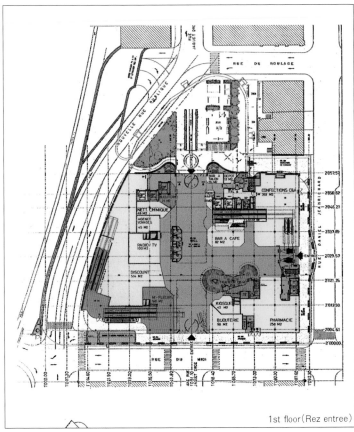

1st floor (Rez entree)

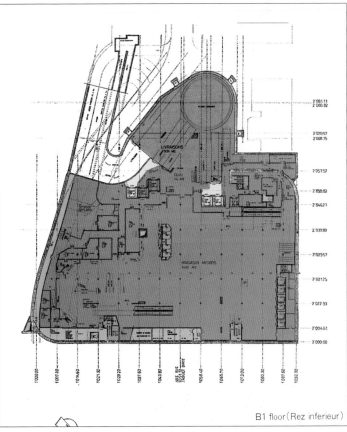

B1 floor (Rez inferieur)

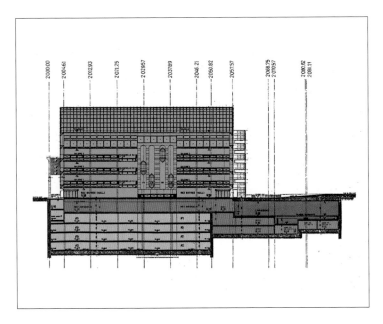

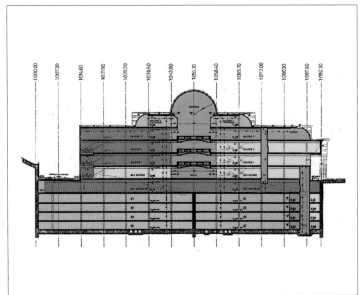

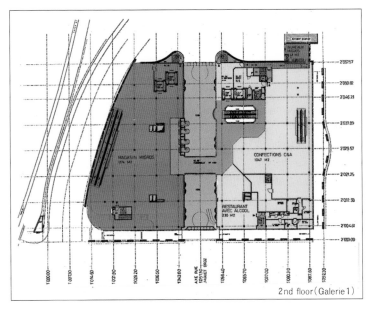

2nd floor (Galerie 1)

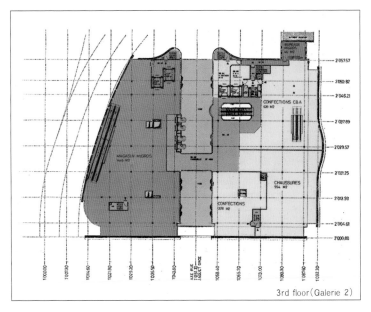

3rd floor (Galerie 2)

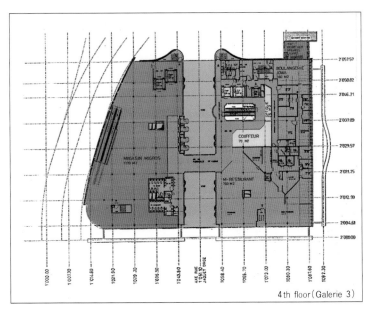

4th floor (Galerie 3)

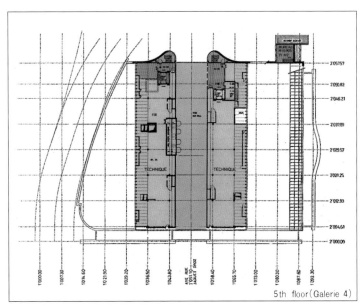

5th floor (Galerie 4)

THE GALLERIA

⟨Hatfield, UK⟩

Totally differing from conventional shopping centers and leisure centers in the U.K., "THE GALLERIA" is Americanized. Situated on a highway tunnel (A1 Road) extending to the north from London, it stands out a great deal. This type of location is very rare even across the world. Structurally, it is characterized by Europe's largest single-spanned mall 145 m in total length and 50 m in width, and the world's highest (25 m) shop windows, and is covered with plate glass. The A1 Road is used by 40 million cars per year and the area within 30 minutes by car of this shopping center has a population of 3 million. Thus, since its commercial territory covers a considerably wide area, this shopping center has a parking space for 2,000 cars. The center court is used for ice skating, various entertainment productions, events, etc., thus serving as the largest feature for capturing shoppers.

● THE GALLERIA
Address: Comet Way Hatfield, Hartfordshire ALIO OXR, UK
Opened: 1992
Developer: Carroll Group
Design: Aukett Ltd.
Area: 35,000 m²
Number of cars parked: 2,200
Key tenants: Lester Bowden
Number of tenants: 130

⟨ザ ギャレリア＝THE GALLERIA⟩は これまでのイギリスのショッピングセンターやレジャーセンターとは全く趣きを異にし アメリカナイズされている。ロンドンから北に延びるモーターウェイ（A１ロード）のトンネル上に立地し とにかくよく目立つ。世界でもこのような立地は珍しい。構造的には 全長145メートル 幅50メートルのシングルスパーンのモール（ヨーローパで最大）と 23メートルという世界一高いショップウインドを持ち 4,185㎡の板ガラスで覆われている。A１ロードは 年間4,000万台の通行量で 車で30分以内の地域には300万人の人口があり 地元Hatfield はもとより 商圏はかなり広範囲に及ぶため このショッピングセンターは 2,000台の駐車スペースを確保している。中央のセンターコートでは アイススケートやファッションショー 各種のエンターテイメント イベントなどが催され 集客の最大のポイントとなっている。

●ザ ギャレリア
住所：   Comet Way Hatfield, Hartfordshire ALIO OXR, UK
開店：   1992年
デベロッパー： Carroll Group
設計：   Aukett Ltd.
面積：   35,000㎡
駐車台数：   2,200
キーテナント： Lester Bowden
テナント数：   130

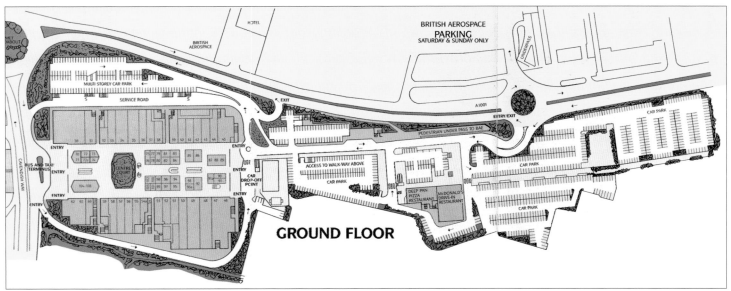

GROUND FLOOR

Lower level

Bus and Taxi Point

Entrance

Carringtons 61-62				70	71	30 Holmes
VACANT 60	104-8			72A	72	31 VACANT
Photo Optix 60A				74	73	Entrance
The Levi Shop 59						32 VACANT
VACANT 58						33 VACANT
Carlton Cards 57	Central Entertainments Area					34 VACANT
Allsports 56						35 VACANT
Thomas Cook 55						36 The Body Shop
Charli Basics 54						37 VACANT
Charli 54	103 100	75-76				38 Oasis
	101 102	78 77				
VACANT 53	99 98	79-80				39 Stylo Barratt
Fashion de Qualita 52	97 96	82 81				40 Our Price
Gooday Leather 51	95 94	84 83				41 Tandy
VACANT 50						42 VACANT
Superdrug 49	93 93A	85				43 VACANT
	92	86				44 Rosebys
First Sport 48	91A	87-89				45 Bell & Crane
Tempo 46-47	91 90					

Entrance   Cashpoint

EL Substation

Car Park 122 Spaces

Entrance

69 Deep Pan Pizza

Entrance

McDonalds 68

Car Park 599 Spaces

Multi-Storey Car Park 1040 Spaces

N

30	Holmes
31	VACANT
32	VACANT
33	VACANT
34	VACANT
35	VACANT
36	The Body Shop
37	VACANT
38	Oasis
39	Stylo Barratt
40	Our Price
41	Tandy
42	VACANT
43	VACANT
44	Rosebys
45	Bell & Crane
46-47	Tempo
48	First Sport
49	Superdrug
50	VACANT
51	Gooday Leather
52	Fashion de Qualita
53	VACANT
54	Charli
54A	Charli Basics
55	Thomas Cook
56	Allsports
57	Carlton Cards
58	VACANT
59	The Levi Shop
60	VACANT
60A	Photo Optix
61-62	Carringtons
68	McDonalds
69	Deep Pan Pizza
70	VACANT
71	VACANT
72	VACANT
72A	VACANT
73	Tennessee Secret
74	Maddisons
75-76	Whittards
77	VACANT
78	BM Jewellers
79-80	The Art & Craft Shop
81	Batya
82	Stencil Store
83	Minds Eye
84	Torq
85	Mondo Pelle
86	Leisure Zone
87-89	Country Secrets
90	Headlines
91	Supercuts
91A	VACANT
92	Penco
93	Shirt
93A	Bear To Be Fitted
94	Knickerbox
95	Knockout Clothing Company
96	Passo Blu
97	Scruples
98	VACANT
99	VACANT
100/102	Big Rock Candy Mountain
101	Lessiters
103	VACANT
104-108	Rendezvous

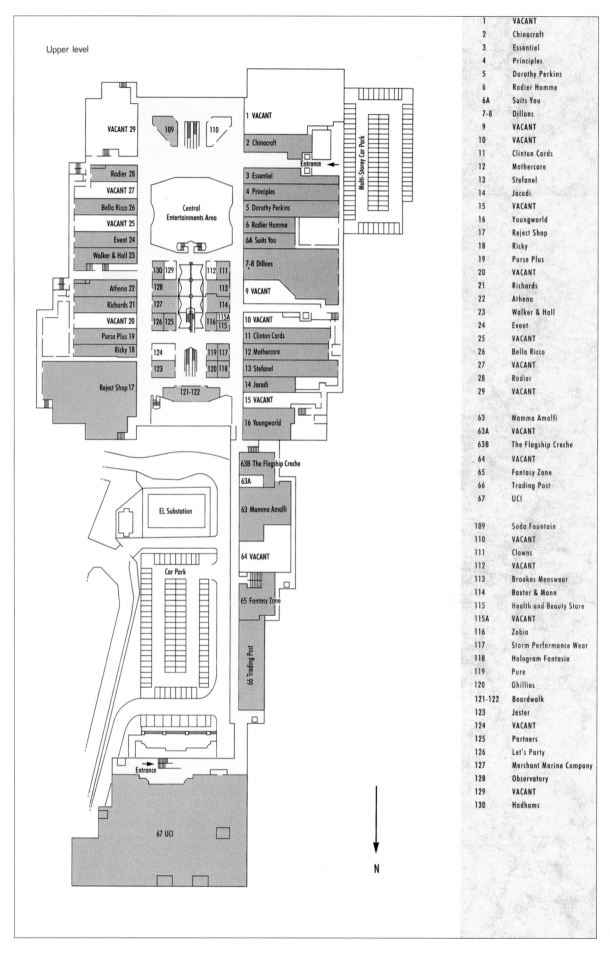

Upper level

1	VACANT
2	Chinacraft
3	Essentiel
4	Principles
5	Dorothy Perkins
6	Rodier Homme
6A	Suits You
7-8	Dillons
9	VACANT
10	VACANT
11	Clinton Cards
12	Mothercare
13	Stefanel
14	Jacadi
15	VACANT
16	Youngworld
17	Reject Shop
18	Ricky
19	Purse Plus
20	VACANT
21	Richards
22	Athena
23	Walker & Hall
24	Event
25	VACANT
26	Bella Ricco
27	VACANT
28	Rodier
29	VACANT
63	Mamma Amalfi
63A	VACANT
63B	The Flagship Creche
64	VACANT
65	Fantasy Zone
66	Trading Post
67	UCI
109	Soda Fountain
110	VACANT
111	Clowns
112	VACANT
113	Brookes Menswear
114	Baxter & Mann
115	Health and Beauty Store
115A	VACANT
116	Zobia
117	Storm Performance Wear
118	Hologram Fantasia
119	Pure
120	Ghillies
121-122	Boardwalk
123	Jester
124	VACANT
125	Partners
126	Let's Party
127	Merchant Marine Company
128	Observatory
129	VACANT
130	Hadhams

ITÄKESKUS

〈Helsinki, Finland〉

"Itäkeskus" meaning an "eastern center" in English, is a bedroom town situated about 8 km east of Helsinki, and blessed with a rich natural environment. At present, there are about 150,000 inhabitants. Since it is directly linked to Helsinki through a subway, its population is expected to increase by about 30% by 2000. Thus, Itäkeskus is the most noticeably developing town in the metropolitan area.

The construction of an extension to "Itäkeskus" was started at the end of 1989 and completed in the fall of 1992. The extension is connected to the original facility through an atrium. With three department stores, "Anttila," "Stockmann" and "CitySokos," as the key tenants, the shopping center is tenanted by a total of 170 shops occupying Scandinavia's largest selling area (80,000 m²). In the center, there is an atrium, 200 m in total length, 16 m in width and 22 m in height, and the selling corners are linked by 6 bridges. Environmental considerations have also been given to the mall space by installing benches, works of art, potted greenery, etc. Thus, the facility is gaining popularity as an oasis for community inhabitants who are less blessed with fine weather, and also as a general living center. The simply and colorfully designed facade gives a fresh impression.

● ITÄKESKUS

Address:	Kauppakeskus Itäkeskus TurunIInnantie 4A SF-00130 Helsinki, Finland
Opened:	November 1992
Developer:	Haka OY., Sponda OY.
Design:	Juhani Pallasmaa, Heikkinen-Komonen OY., Helin & Siitonen Hyvämäki-Karhunen-Parkkinen, Häkli & Karhunen
Area:	80,000 m²
Number of cars parked:	2,500
Key tenants:	Anttila, Stockmann, CitySokos
Number of tenants:	170

英語でイースタンセンターを意味する イテケスクス(Itäkeskus)は ヘルシンキの東 約8キロに位置するベッドタウンで 現在 周辺には約15万人が居住している。ヘルシンキとは地下鉄で直結されている便利性もあり 2000年には 約30%の人口増が見込まれ 首都圏でも最も著しい発展が見られる場所である。この〈イテケスクス=ITÄKESKUS〉は 1989年末から拡張工事に入り1992年秋に完成した。〈Anttila〉〈Stockmann〉〈CitySokos〉の 3つの百貨店をキーテナントに トータル170店で構成され 売り場面積 80,000㎡という北欧一の規模を誇っている。中央部分に全長200メートル 幅16メートル 高さ22メートルのアトリウムを設け 6ケ所のブリッジで各売り場を結んでいる。モール内にはベンチやオブジェ 植栽など 環境面の配慮もなされ あまり天候に恵まれないこの地方の オアシスとして また 総合生活センターとして地元市民の人気を得ている。

● イテケスクス

住所：	Kauppakeskus Itäkeskus TurunIInnantie 4A SF-00130 Helsinki, Finland
開店：	1992年11月
デベロッパー：	Haka OY., Sponda OY.
設計：	Juhani Pallasmaa, Heikkinen-Komonen OY., Helin & Siitonen, Hyvämäki-Karhunen-Parkkinen, Häkli & Karhunen
面積：	80,000㎡
駐車台数：	2,500
キーテナント：	Anttila, Stockmann, CitySokos
テナント数：	170

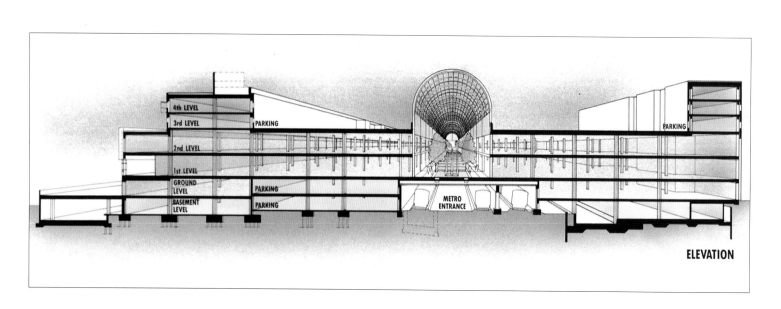

ELEVATION

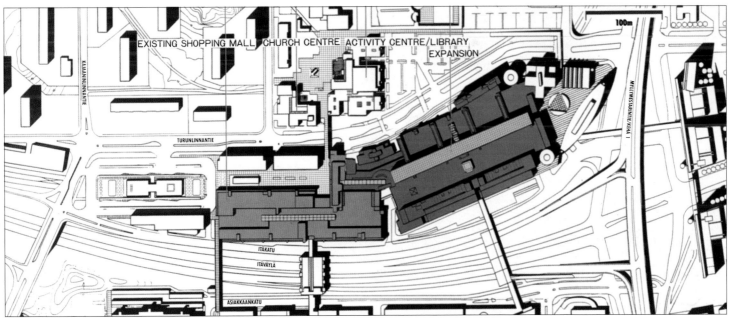

EXISTING SHOPPING MALL CHURCH CENTRE ACTIVITY CENTRE/LIBRARY
EXPANSION

KAJAANINLINNANTIE

TURUNLINNANTIE

ITAKATU

ITAVAYLA

ASIAKKAANKATU

MYLLYMESTARINTIE/KEHA 1

100m

MIGRATING BIRDS
OLIVIER MOURGUE 92.

OLIVIER MOURGUE 92

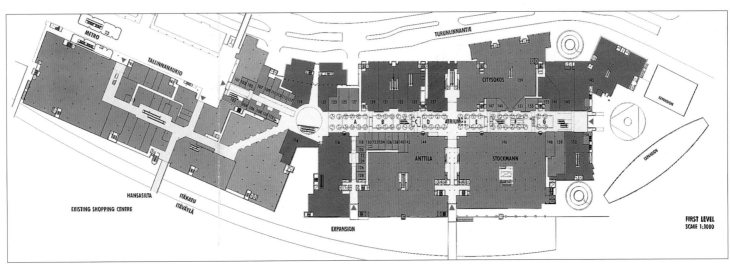

METRO

TURUNLINNANTIE

TALLINNANAUKIO

CITYSOKOS   139

ATRIUM

EXPANSION

ANTTILA   STOCKMANN

HANSASILTA   ITÄKATU
EXISTING SHOPPING CENTRE   ITÄVÄYLÄ

EXPANSION

FIRST LEVEL
SCALE 1:1000

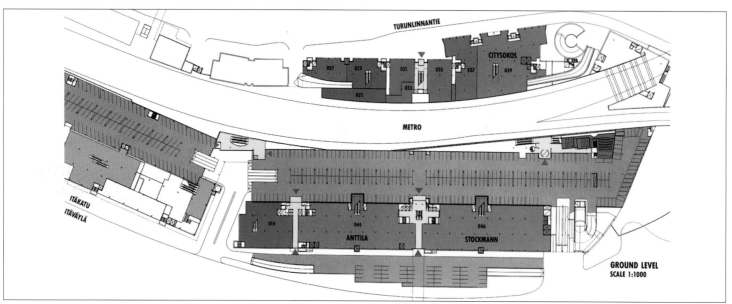

TURUNLINNANTIE

CITYSOKOS

027 029 031 035 037 039
025 033

METRO

ITÄKATU
ITÄVÄYLÄ

016 044 046
ANTTILA STOCKMANN

GROUND LEVEL
SCALE 1:1000

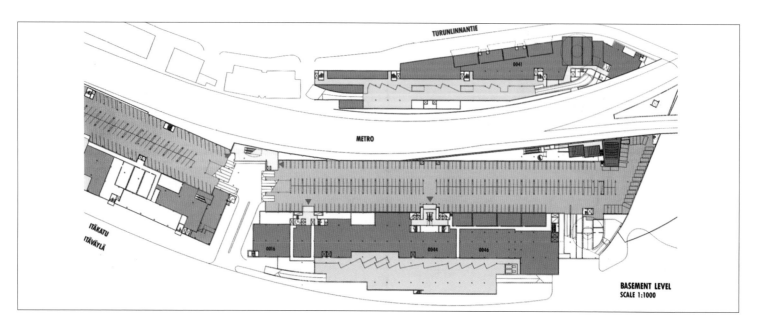

TURUNLINNANTIE

0041

METRO

ITÄKATU
ITÄVÄYLÄ

0016 0044 0046

BASEMENT LEVEL
SCALE 1:1000

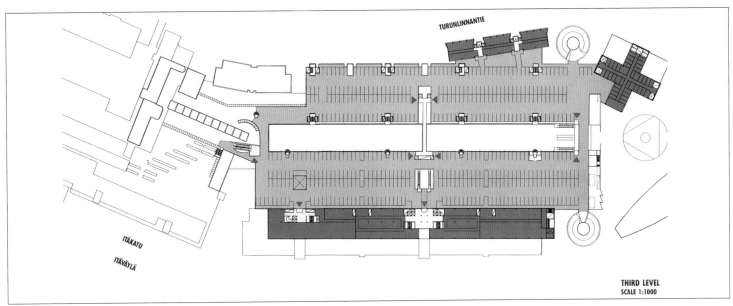

TURUNLINNANTIE

ITÄKATU

ITÄVÄYLÄ

THIRD LEVEL
SCALE 1:1000

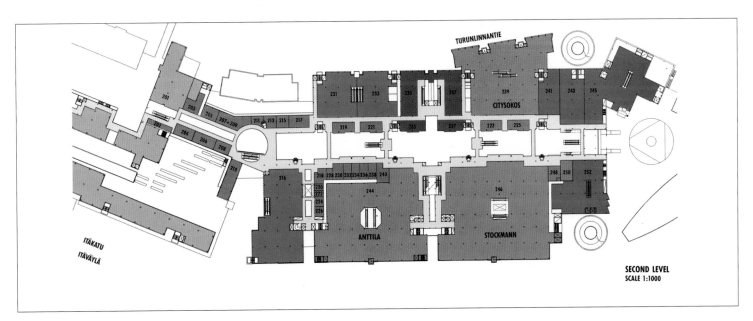

TURUNLINNANTIE

201
203
205
207+209
202
204
206
208
210
211 213 215 217
219 221
216
218 228 230 232 234 236 238 240
220
222
224
226
244
231 233 235 237
239
CITYSOKOS
241 243 245
223 225
237
246
248 250 252
ANTTILA
STOCKMANN

ITÄKATU

ITÄVÄYLÄ

SECOND LEVEL
SCALE 1:1000

MONUMENT MALL

⟨Newcastle, UK⟩

Opened in Newcastle, the largest commercial city in the north-eastern part of England, this shopping center is finished in the Victorian style, and the domed facade is designed in the image of the city's golden agé when it flourished as a commercial and industrial center and as a trading port. The shopping center is situated in the central area of the city facing the monument tower of the well known tea brand "Earl Grey," and is connected by a tunnel to the main subway station, Monument Station. About 220,000 passengers enter and exit the station every week. There are about one million inhabitants within the territory of this shopping center. As a port town, Newcastle also has shipping lanes leading to Scandinavia across the North Sea, and thus has a favorable background for capturing shoppers.

Under the domed atrium there are see-through elevators and escalators connecting the floors. The 4-storied arcade is designed so that the higher the floor, the further back the shop-front line is, thus allowing more light to come in, and one can enjoy a view of the atrium's dome from every floor. All the floors are finished with mosaicked terrazzo, while metallic handrails are generally curved in sharp contrast to the vertical lighted columns. The uppermost parts of the atrium and arcade walls are decorated with illustrations of the farmer's daughter and Scottish prince of the Scandinavian legend "North Sea Saga." Etched glass illustrations are also used. Thus, the interior decorations fully utilize traditional crafts.

● MONUMENT MALL

Address:	Nothumberland St./ Blackett St. Newcastle Upon Tyne, UK
Opened:	June 3, 1992
Developer:	St. Martins Property Cooperation Ltd.
Design:	Hugh Martin Partnership
Area:	11,500 m²
Number of cars parked:	0

イギリス北東部最大の商業都市 ニューカッスル(Newcastle) にオープンしたこのショッピングセンターはヴィクトリア時代の様式で ドームのあるファサードは 商工業と貿易港として最も潤った 黄金時代をイメージしてデザインされている。茶の銘柄として有名なアール グレー(Earl Grey)のモニュメントタワーに面した 中心部に立地し 地下鉄の中枢 Monument 駅とは地下で結ばれている。この駅の乗降客は週22万人で 圏内の居住者は約100万人 また港町として 北海を隔てたスカンジナビアへの航路も開かれており集客には絶好の背景にある。ドームのアトリウムの下にはシースルーのエレベーターとエスカレーターが各フロアを結び 4層になったアーケードは上層階ほど店頭のラインをステップバックさせているので 採光性に優れ どの階からもアトリウムのドームが見通せる。床は各階ともテラゾーのモザイク模様 手すりはメタルで全体にカーブを持たせ 照明が取り付けられた柱の垂直なラインとは対照的である。 アトリウムとアーケードの最上部の壁面には 北海の伝説 "Norht Sea Saga" にまつわる百姓娘とスコットランド王子のイラストが描かれている。またエッチドグラスのイラストなど すみずみまでクラフトの伝統が活かされている。

● モニュメント モール

住所:	Nothumberland St./Blackett St. Newcastle Upon Tyne, UK
開店:	1992年6月3日
デベロッパー:	St. Martins Property Cooporation Ltd.
設計:	Hugh Martin Partnership
面積:	11,500m²
駐車台数:	0
キーテナント:	Burton, Virgin Megastore, Boots, Benetton, Body Shop
テナント数:	46

Key tenants:	Burton, Virgin Megastore, Boots, Benetton, Body Shop
Number of tenants:	46

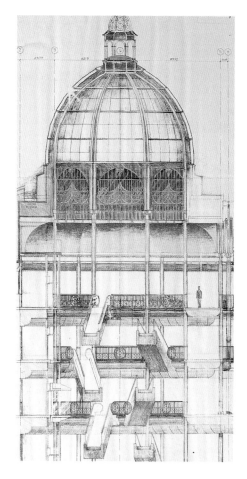

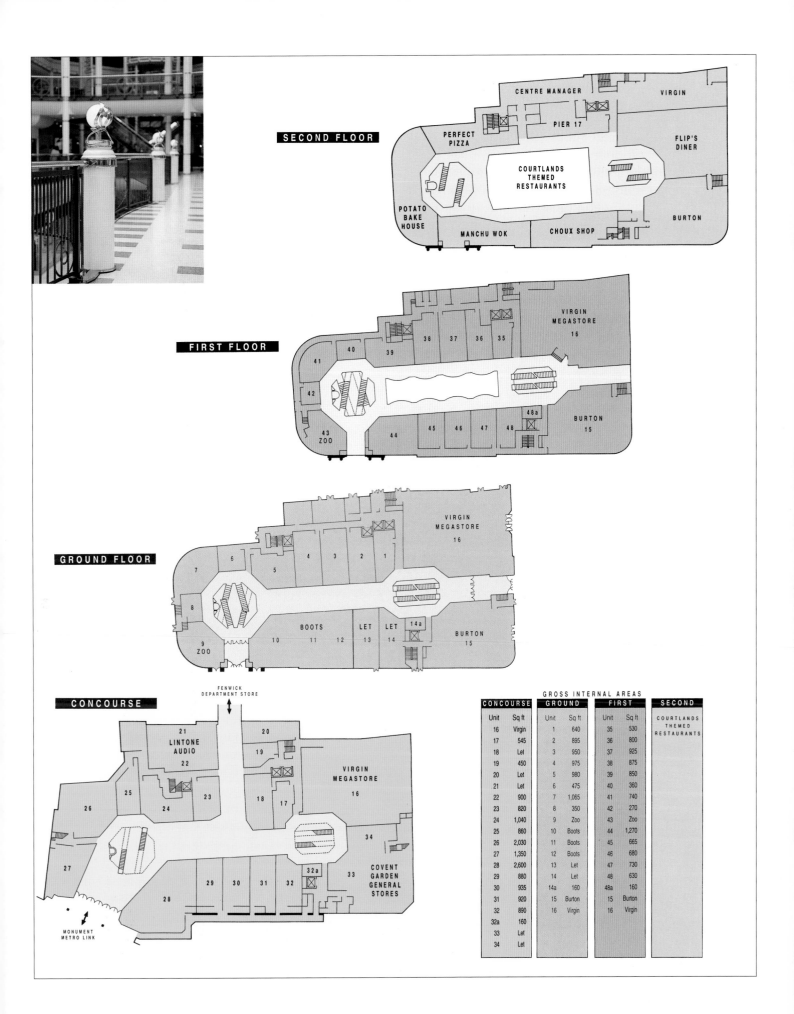

SECOND FLOOR

CENTRE MANAGER · VIRGIN · PIER 17 · FLIP'S DINER · PERFECT PIZZA · COURTLANDS THEMED RESTAURANTS · POTATO BAKE HOUSE · MANCHU WOK · CHOUX SHOP · BURTON

FIRST FLOOR

VIRGIN MEGASTORE 16 · BURTON 15 · ZOO 43 · 35 36 37 38 39 40 41 42 44 45 46 47 48 48a

GROUND FLOOR

VIRGIN MEGASTORE 16 · BOOTS · LET · LET · 14a · BURTON 15 · ZOO 9 · 1 2 3 4 5 6 7 8 10 11 12 13 14

CONCOURSE

FENWICK DEPARTMENT STORE · LINTONE AUDIO · VIRGIN MEGASTORE 16 · COVENT GARDEN GENERAL STORES · MONUMENT METRO LINK

GROSS INTERNAL AREAS

CONCOURSE		GROUND		FIRST		SECOND
Unit	Sq ft	Unit	Sq ft	Unit	Sq ft	COURTLANDS THEMED RESTAURANTS
16	Virgin	1	640	35	530	
17	545	2	895	36	800	
18	Let	3	950	37	925	
19	450	4	975	38	875	
20	Let	5	980	39	850	
21	Let	6	475	40	360	
22	900	7	1,065	41	740	
23	820	8	350	42	270	
24	1,040	9	Zoo	43	Zoo	
25	860	10	Boots	44	1,270	
26	2,030	11	Boots	45	665	
27	1,350	12	Boots	46	680	
28	2,600	13	Let	47	730	
29	880	14	Let	48	630	
30	935	14a	160	48a	160	
31	920	15	Burton	15	Burton	
32	890	16	Virgin	16	Virgin	
32a	160					
33	Let					
34	Let					

THOMAS NEAL'S

⟨London, UK⟩

The triangular area called the "Seven Dials Monument," and surrounded by Neals Street, Earlmam Street and Shorts Gardens, is a place where many breweries moved and built warehouses. As such, it is a relatively historical place even in the Covent Garden area.

This complex opened in May 1992 as a result of redevelopment, and is composed of 29 retail shops, 3 restaurants, 4 offices, and 15 residential units. The medieval building is characterized by modern artistic and craft-like designs, and round mosaic patterns designed by Jennefer Durran are painted on the floor. Various types of materials are used for finish, including steel, brass, copper, stained glass and York stone, and the interior space is accented with craft-like works of art using Victorian characters as their motif. The arcade under the bricked tunnel connecting Shorts Gardens and Earlham Street, called "Cucumber Alley," has a row of small unique shops, creating an atmosphere characteristic of London.

● THOMAS NEAL'S

Address: Neals Street Covent Garden London WC2, UK
Opened: May 1, 1992
Developer: Kleinwort Benson Trustees
Design: RHWL Partnership, Chris Maton
Area: 40,050 m²
Number of cars parked: 0
Key tenants: Space NK, Mezzaluna
Number of tenants: 32

ロンドンで Seven Dials Monumennt と呼ばれている Neal ストリートと Earlmam ストリート Shorts Gardens に囲まれたトライアングル地域は 19世紀に多くの醸造所が移転し そのための倉庫が建てられていた処で コベントガーデン（Covent Garden）地区でも歴史のある場所である。再開発されて 1992年5月にオープンしたこのコンプレックスは 29店のリテイルショップ 3店のレストラン オフィス 4 住居ユニット 15で 構成されている。中世風の建物は モダーンアートとクラフト的なデザインが特徴で 床には Jennefer Durran のデザインによる円形のモザイク模様が描かれている。仕上げ材料には スチール ブラス 銅 ステンドグラス ヨークストーンなど多くのマテリアルが使用され ヴィクトリア時代のキャラクターをモチーフにしたクラフト的なオブジェが目につく。Shorts Gardens と Earlham ストリートを結ぶレンガづくりのヴォルトの下のアーケードは "キューカンバー アレ（Cucumber Alle）" と呼ばれ 小さな個性的な店舗が並び いかにもロンドンらしい雰囲気である。

● トーマス ニールス

住所： Neals Street Covent Garden London WC2, UK
開店： 1992年5月1日
デベロッパー： Kleinwort Benson Trustees
設計： RHWL Partnership, Chris Maton
面積： 40,050㎡
駐車台数： 0
キーテナント： Space NK, Mezzaluna
テナント数： 32

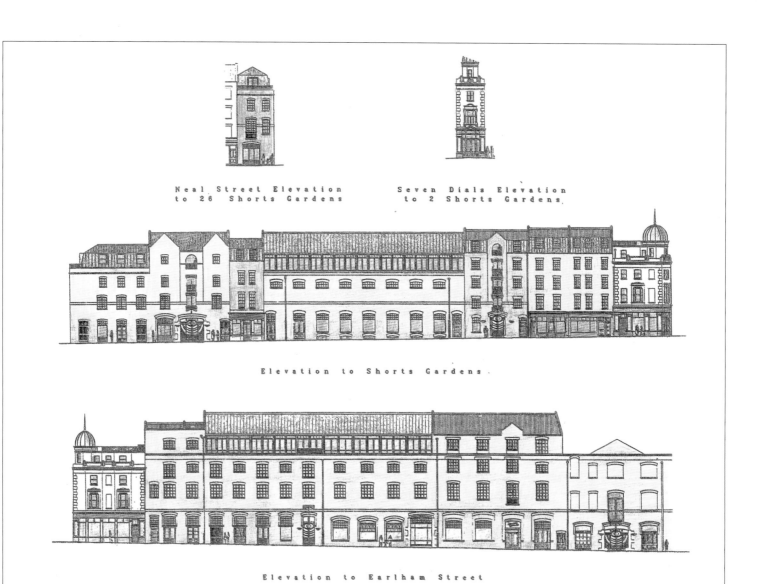

Neal Street Elevation
to 26 Shorts Gardens

Seven Dials Elevation
to 2 Shorts Gardens.

Elevation to Shorts Gardens.

Elevation to Earlham Street

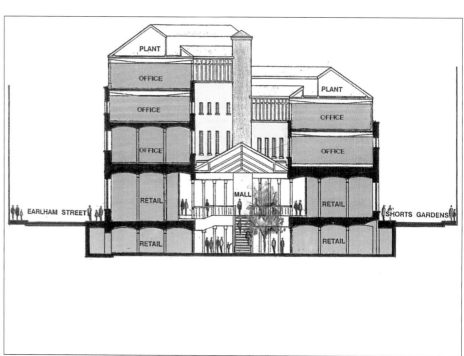

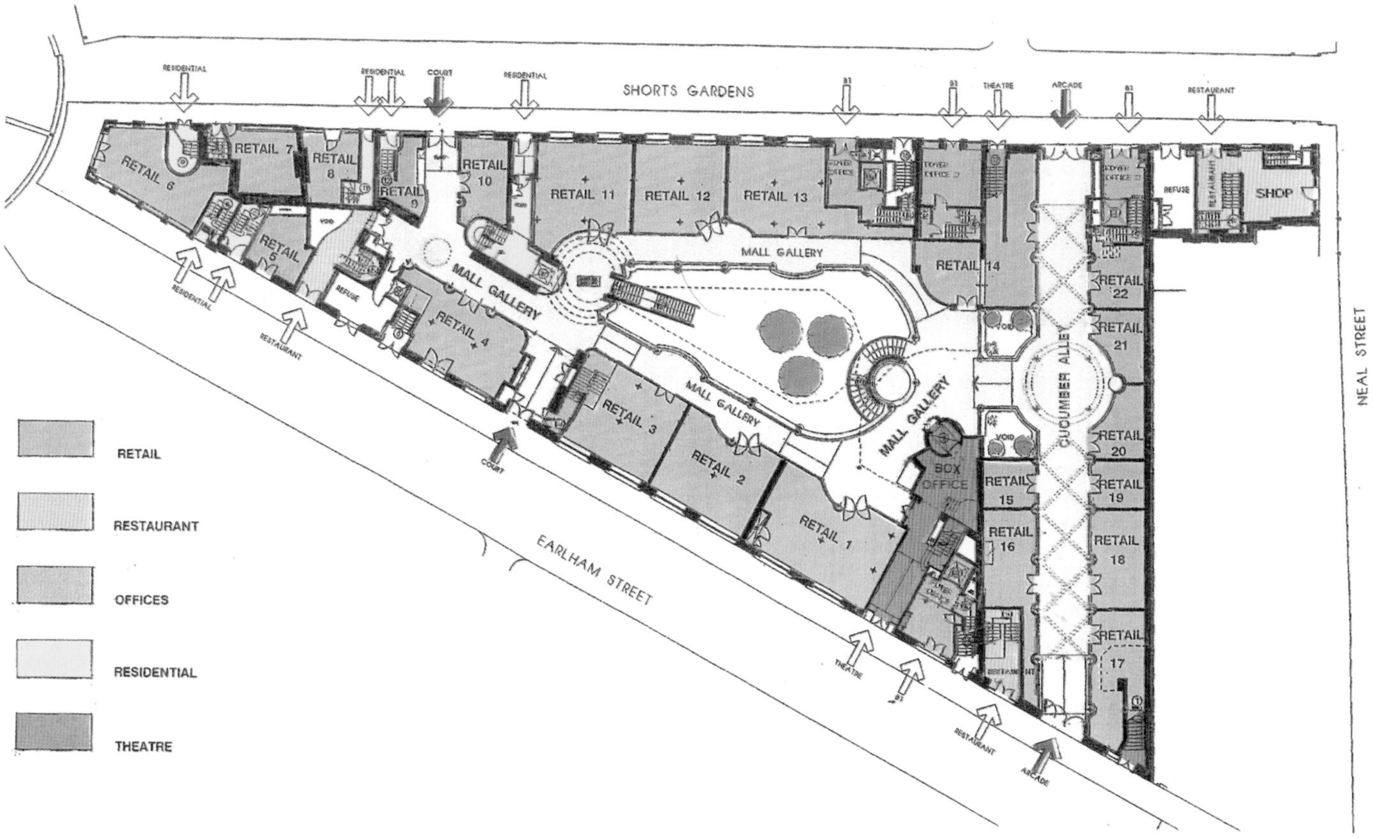

SHORTS GARDENS
EARLHAM STREET
NEAL STREET
CUCUMBER ALLEY
MALL GALLERY
BOX OFFICE
RETAIL 1
RETAIL 2
RETAIL 3
RETAIL 4
RETAIL 5
RETAIL 6
RETAIL 7
RETAIL 8
RETAIL 9
RETAIL 10
RETAIL 11
RETAIL 12
RETAIL 13
RETAIL 14
RETAIL 15
RETAIL 16
RETAIL 17
RETAIL 18
RETAIL 19
RETAIL 20
RETAIL 21
RETAIL 22
SHOP
RESIDENTIAL
COURT
THEATRE
ARCADE
RESTAURANT
RETAIL
RESTAURANT
OFFICES
RESIDENTIAL
THEATRE

GROUND FLOOR PLAN

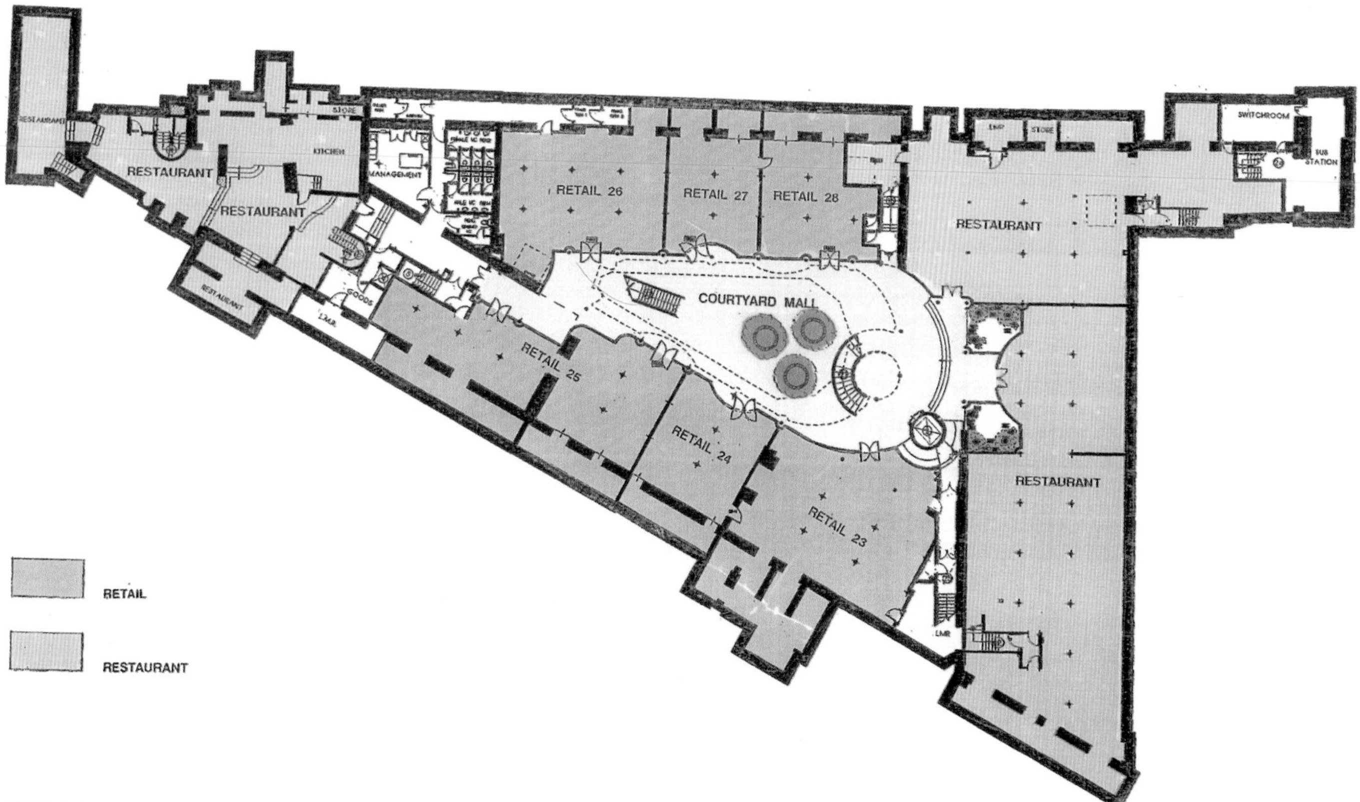

COURTYARD MALL
RESTAURANT
KITCHEN
MANAGEMENT
STORE
SWITCHROOM
RETAIL 23
RETAIL 24
RETAIL 25
RETAIL 26
RETAIL 27
RETAIL 28
RETAIL
RESTAURANT

BASEMENT PLAN

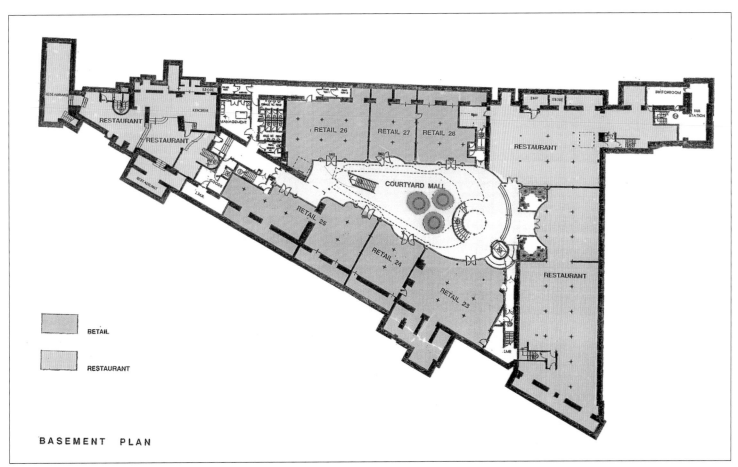

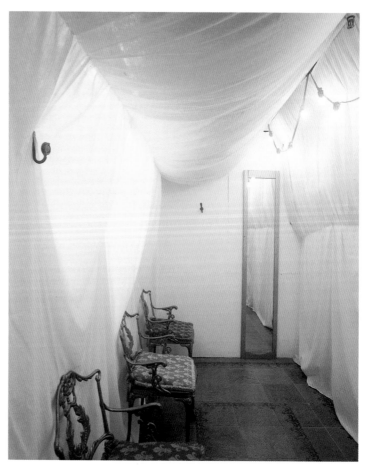

CENTRE COURT

〈Wimbledon, UK〉

Wimbledon is very well known as the town where the British Open Tennis Tournament is held, but it is also a high-class bedroom town for London. This facility whose name, "CENTRE COURT," comes from the court where the final game is held, is a station building type shopping center directly connecting British Rail to Wimbledon Station. It has been developed while preserving historical buildings such as the Town Hall constructed in the 1930s, the Edwardian Fire Station, and the Baptist Church. The newly constructed building adjoining the Town Hall which, in turn, connects to the station, has two levels whose total area is about 30,000 m². With "Debenhams" (department store) as the key tenant, it is composed of 48 shops including "Boots," "Marks & Spencer," "Mothercare" and "Richards." The Town Hall is tenanted by 19 shops on the two levels, with the former conference room on the upper level having been renovated into a tea room.

●CENTRE COURT

Address: The Broadway Wimbledon London SW19, UK
Opened: September 17, 1992
Developer: Speyhawk Retail plc. Standard Life
Design: Building Design Partnership
Area: 30,000 m²
Number of cars parked: 770
Key tenants: Debenhams, Boots, Marks & Spencer, Mothercare, Richards
Number of tenants: 67

ウインブルドンは テニスの全英オープンが行われる町としてあまりにも有名であるが ロンドンの高級ベッドタウンでもある。〈センター コート＝CENTRE COURT〉の店名は その決勝戦の行われるコートに由来したもので 英国鉄（British Rail）と地下鉄のウインブルドン駅に直結した 駅ビル型のショッピングセンターである。開発にあたっては 1930年代に建造されたタウンホール（Town Hall）や消防署（Edwardian Fire Station）バプチスト教会（Baptist Church）などの歴史的な建物を残し進められた。駅に隣接するタウンホールにジョイントして新築された建物は 2層で 総面積が約30,000㎡。〈Debenhams〉（百貨店）をキーテナントにして〈Boots〉〈Marks & Spencer〉〈Mothercare〉〈Richards〉など48店で構成。タウンホールは2層で19店のテナント 上階の旧 会議室は ティールームにリニューアルされた。

●センター コート

住所： The Broadway Wimbledon London SW19, UK
開店： 1992年 9月17日
デベロッパー：Speyhawk Retail plc. Standard Life
設計： Building Design Partnership
面積： 30,000㎡
駐車台数： 770
キーテナント：Debenhams, Boots, Marks & Spencer, Mothercare, Richards
テナント数： 67

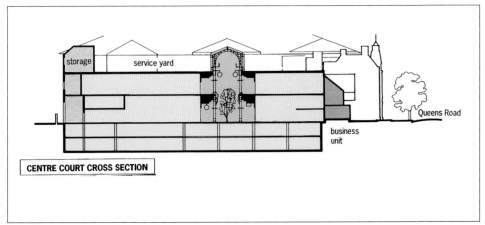

storage   service yard

Queens Road

business
unit

CENTRE COURT CROSS SECTION

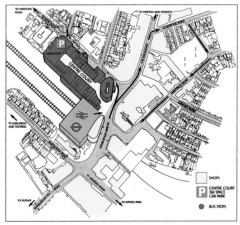

UPPER SHOPPING LEVEL

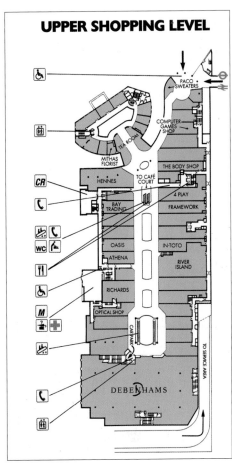

LOWER SHOPPING LEVEL

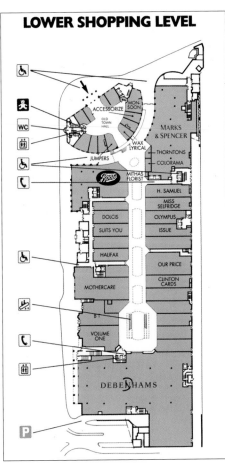

THE PEACOCKS

⟨Woking, UK⟩

About 45 km to the southwest of London and connected by a railway and highway, Woking is developing as a bedroom town for London. Since it is situated at the midpoint between Heathrow Airport and Gatwick Airport, it is also drawing attention as an office town. As part of the project for developing the northern side of Woking Station of British Railway, the southwestern part of the Town Square was redeveloped into "THE PEACOCKS" which opened in 1992.

The facility has about 45,000 m² in total area, with the shopping center installed side by side with a public hall, a theater, a night club, a library, offices, etc.

"THE PEACOCKS" is an atrium-type facility with 4 levels, and a total selling space of 29,000 m² which is tenanted by 65 shops in total, centering around large shops such as "Allders," "Marks & Spencer" and "C & A." In the commercial territory of Woking there are 870,000 inhabitants within 20 minutes and 2,550,000 people within 30 minutes of this facility. For shoppers driving cars, there is a parking area for 2,400 vehicles.

● THE PEACOCKS

Address:	Center of Woking, UK
Opened:	1992
Developer:	London & Edinburgh Trust, Woking Borough Council
Design:	Chapman Taylor Partners
Area:	29,000 m²
Number of cars parked:	2,400
Key tenants:	Allders, Marks & Spencer, C & A
Number of tenants:	65

ロンドンの南西に約45キロ 鉄道及びハイウェイ網で結ばれた ウォキング(Woking)は ロンドンのベッドタウンとして発展しているが ヒースロー空港(Heathrow airport)と ガドウィック空港(Gatwick airport)の中間地点にあたるため オフィスタウンとしても注目されているところである。英国鉄(Buritish Railway)の ウォキング駅北側開発の一環で タウン スクウェア(Town Squear)の西南部を再開発しオープンしたもの。
その規模は ショッピングセンターと公会堂 劇場 ナイトクラブ 図書館 オフィスなどを併設した 延面積45,000㎡に及ぶ。
4層で アトリウム形式の〈ザ ピーコックス=THE PEACOKS〉は〈Allders〉と〈Marks & Spencer〉〈C & A〉などの大型ショップを核に 合計65店のテナント 29,000㎡の売場面積で構成されている。ウォキングの商圏には20分以内に87万人 30分以内には 255万人が居住し 車による利用客のために 2,400台収容のパーキングスペースを確保している。

● ザ ピーコックス

住所：	Center of Woking, UK
開店：	1992年
デベロッパー：	London & Edinburgh Trust, Woking Borough Council
設計：	Chapman Taylor Partners
面積：	29,000㎡
駐車台数：	2,400
キーテナント：	Allders, Marks & Spencer, C & A
テナント数：	65

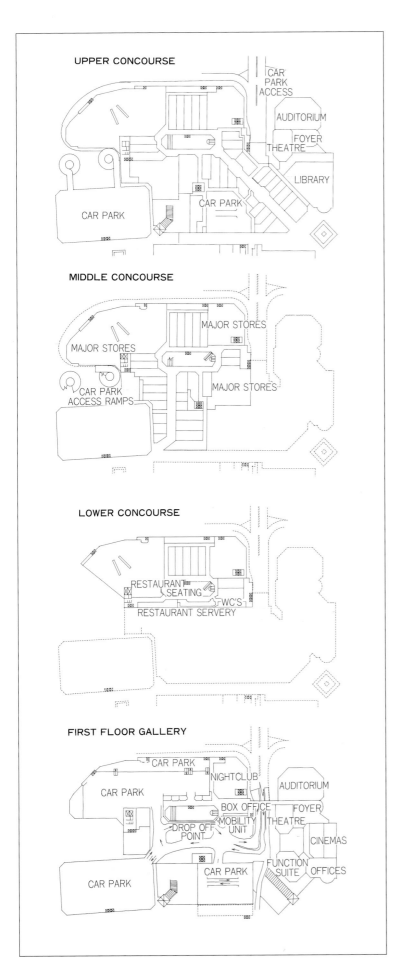

UPPER CONCOURSE

CAR PARK ACCESS
AUDITORIUM
FOYER
THEATRE
LIBRARY
CAR PARK
CAR PARK

MIDDLE CONCOURSE

MAJOR STORES
MAJOR STORES
CAR PARK ACCESS RAMPS
MAJOR STORES

LOWER CONCOURSE

RESTAURANT SEATING
WC'S
RESTAURANT SERVERY

FIRST FLOOR GALLERY

CAR PARK
NIGHTCLUB
CAR PARK
AUDITORIUM
BOX OFFICE
FOYER
DROP OFF POINT
MOBILITY UNIT
THEATRE
CINEMAS
FUNCTION SUITE
OFFICES
CAR PARK
CAR PARK

THE GALLERIES
〈Bristol, UK〉

Bristol is the second largest financial city in the U.K., next only to London. In 1940, its central area was destroyed by a surprise attack by German forces, and was restored after the war. This shopping center opened in October 1991 as part of the renewal of the Broadmead area where multi-purpose buildings are located. It has an area of 22,000 m² and thus can be counted among the five largest facilities in the U.K. In constructing this shopping center, £120 million (about ¥40 billion) were invested, and 1,250,000 bricks, 3,180 m² of plate glass and 10,000 m³ of concrete were used. The glass-roofed building with an atrium is composed of 3 levels, and the 1st, 2nd and 3rd floors are called "Broad Mead," "Union Gallery" and "Castel Gallery," respectively, and are tenanted by 120 shops in total. "The Alms House" on the Merchant Street side, which faces this complex, was formerly a pension, but was renovated into a cafe, wine bar & restaurant which harmonizes well with the glazing of the shopping center.

●THE GALLERIES
Address: The Broadmead, Bristol, UK
Opened: October 1991
Developer: Norwich Union, Ladboke Group
Design: Crighton Mc Coll, Leslie Jones
Area: 32,000 m²
Number of cars parked: 1,100
Key tenants: Boots, WH Smith, Waterstones
Number of tenants: 120

ブリストルは ロンドンに次ぐイギリス第2の金融都市で その中心部は1940年にドイツ軍の奇襲攻撃で消失し戦後復興した。このショッピングセンターは雑居ビルが建ち並ぶブロードミード（Broadmead）地区の再開発により 1991年10月にオープンしたもので 規模は22,000㎡と 英国では五指に数えられる広さである。125万個のレンガと 3,180㎡の板ガラス 10,000㎡のコンクリートが使用され 1億2,000万ポンド（約400億円）の資金が投資された。ガラス屋根でアトリウムのある建物は3層で構成され 1階が "Broad Mead" 2階が "Union Gallery" 3階が "Castel Gallery" と各々の名称で呼ばれ120店のテナントで構成している。このコンプレックスが面している マーチャンストリート側の建物 アルムハウス＝The Alms House〉は 元はペンションだったが カフェ ワインバー＆レストランにリニューアルされ ショッピングセンターのガラスの外観に包まれるかたちで うまく溶け込んでいる。

●ザ ギャラリーズ
住所： The Broadmead, Bristol, UK
開店： 1991年10月
デベロッパー： Norwich Union, Ladboke Group
設計： Crighton Mc Coll, Leslie Jones
面積： 32,000㎡
駐車台数： 1,100
キーテナント： Boots, WH Smith, Waterstones
テナント数： 120

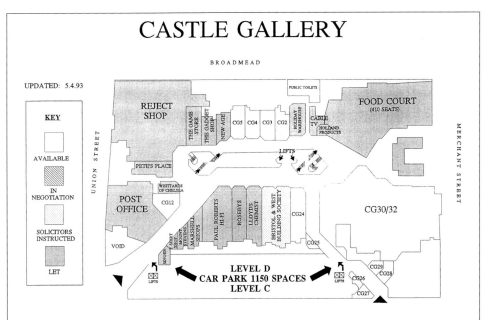

CASTLE GALLERY

BROADMEAD

UPDATED: 5.4.93

KEY

☐ AVAILABLE

▨ IN NEGOTIATION

▨ SOLICITORS INSTRUCTED

▨ LET

UNION STREET

MERCHANT STREET

PUBLIC TOILETS

REJECT SHOP

THE GAME STORE · THE GADGET SHOP · NEW AGE · CG5 · CG4 · CG3 · CG2 · HOLIDAY WAREHOUSE · CABLE TV · HOLLAND PRODUCTS

FOOD COURT (410 SEATS)

PETE'S PLACE

LIFTS

WHITTARDS OF CHELSEA

POST OFFICE

CG12

SINGER · SHOP · MOORE · STEVENS · MARSHALL SHOPS · PAUL ROBERTS HI-FI · ROSEBYS · LLOYDS CHEMIST · BRISTOL & WEST BUILDING SOCIETY · CG24

CG30/32

VOID

CG25

LIFTS

CG29 · CG28

LEVEL D
CAR PARK 1150 SPACES
LEVEL C

CG26

CG27

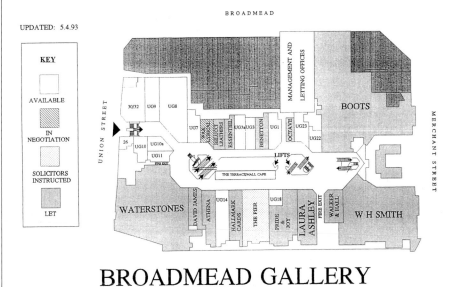

UNION GALLERY

BROADMEAD

UPDATED: 5.4.93

KEY

☐ AVAILABLE

▨ IN NEGOTIATION

▨ SOLICITORS INSTRUCTED

▨ LET

UNION STREET

MERCHANT STREET

MANAGEMENT AND LETTING OFFICES

BOOTS

30/32 · UG9 · UG8

UG7 · BELTS & BUCKLES · BELICHA LEATHERS · UG3a UG3 · BENETTON · OCTAVE · UG23 · UG22 · UG1

26 · UG10 · UG10a · UG11

FIRE EXIT

LIFTS

THE TERRACE/MALL CAFE

WATERSTONES

DAVID JAMES · ATHENA · UG14 · HALLMARK CARDS · THE PIER · UG18 · PRIDE & JOY · LAURA ASHLEY · FIRE EXIT · WALKER & HALL

W H SMITH

BROADMEAD GALLERY

BROADMEAD

UPDATED: 5.4.93

KEY

☐ AVAILABLE

▨ IN NEGOTIATION

▨ SOLICITORS INSTRUCTED

▨ LET

UNION STREET

MERCHANT STREET

THOMAS COOK · IN TOTO · THE GAP · H SAMUEL · CLINTONS · PRINCIPLES · CURTESS · DOLCIS · NEXT · WALLIS · GREYHOUND WALK · SALISBURY · PRINCIPLES MAN · DASH · OLYMPUS

BG10

BG9

PILOT

PACO

LEVIS

OPTIKA

BODY REFORM

FOOTLOCKER

FIRE EXIT

TWINMAR

BG7B

COOKIE JAR · BIRTHDAY · TORQ · DAY TRADING · ALLSPORTS · THE SWEATER SHOP · STEFANEL

BOOTS

FIRE EXIT

BG30 · 23

25

BG31

THE ALMSHOUSE

BRASSERIE

WOOLWORTHS

P.O.

HAMELLS · MARK ONE · ADAMS · OUR PRICE · EARLY LEARNING CENTRES · CIRO CITTERIO · ISSUE · BG26

WH SMITH

DONUT CITY

15/17

ABBEY NATIONAL

LIFTS

KURFÜRSTEN GALERIE
⟨Kassel, Germany⟩

There is an office and residential quarter near Könings Plats in the center of Kassel City which is situated in the central part of Germany and has a population of about 200,000. By spending 130 million German Mark (about ¥9 billion) in construction, this quarter was redeveloped into the "KURFÜRSTEN GALERIE." It is adjoined by a hotel with 128 rooms and banquet and conference halls. The mall features a long L-shaped arcade centering around the dome, with the upper and lower floors linked by escalators at two places. The eastern entrance, which is totally finished with half mirrors, is equipped with elevators leading to a cafe bar on the upper floor. The core tenants, the "Möbenpick Hotel" and the "Marché Restaurant," are in the center of the 1st floor. At each of the two corners beneath the escalators, a flower shop is installed to create a gentle atmosphere on the floor which tends to give hard impressions. The southern main entrance is designed in an art deco style by using plate glass and metal elements, thus expressing a fine contrast with the hotel's exterior wall, which is covered with orange marble.

● KURFÜRSTEN GALERIE
Address: Verwaltungsgesellschaft GmbH Kölnische Strasse 6 D-3500 Kassel, Germany
Opened: September 26, 1991
Developer: Brand Kasse (Kassel), Lebensversicherung AG (Nürnberger)
Design: Planbüro Dipl-Ing, M. Bode
Area: 10,000 m²
Number of cars parked: 530
Key tenants: Kaufhaus, Brinkmann, Möbenpic Hotel, Marché Restaurant
Number of tenants: 30

⟨コールフーシュテン ガレリー＝KURFÜRSTEN GALERIE⟩はドイツ中央部に位置する 人口約20万人のカッセル(Kassel)市の中心部 Könings Plats に近いオフィス兼住宅街を 1億3千万ドイツマルク（約90億円）の工費て再開発したもので 客室数128と 宴会 会議場を有するホテルを併設している。モールはドームを中心にL字型の長いアーケードで 上下階は2ケ所にあるエスカレーターにより連結されている。全面ハーフミラー張りの東側のエントランスには エレベーターが設置され 上階のカフェバーと直結している。核テナントとしては ⟨モーベンピック ホテル＝Möbenpick Hotel⟩ と ⟨マルシェ レストラン＝Marché Restaurant⟩ が 1階中央にある。エスカレーター下のコーナーには2ケ所のフラワーショップを設け ハードになりがちなフロアを 優しさのある雰囲気に演出している。南側のメインエントランスは 板ガラスとメタルでアートデコ調にまとめ オレンジ系大理石で覆ったホテルの外壁とのコントラストを見事に表現している。

● コールフーシュテン ガレリー
住所： Verwaltungsgesellschaft GmbH Kölnische Strasse 6 D-3500 Kassel, Germany
開店： 1991年9月26日
デベロッパー：Brand Kasse (Kassel), Lebensversicherung AG (Nürnberger)
設計： Planbüro Dipl-Ing, M. Bode
面積： 10,000㎡
駐車数： 530
キーテナント：Kaufhaus, Brinkmann, Möbenpic Hotel, Marché Restaurant
テナント数： 30

THE GLADES

⟨Bromley, UK⟩

Situated about 18 km to the southeast of London, Bromley is a town with a population of 300,000. "THE GLADES" was opened by totally developing an area of about 45,000 m² in the center of the town, together with residential units, a church and a leisure center. Consisting of an upper mall level and a lower mall level, it is tenanted by 135 shops in total, centering around "Boots," "Debenhams," "Marks & Spencer" and "Littlewoods." 6 fast food shops, all differing in style, and a food court with 330 seats are located in "Regent Arcade," and are gaining popularity. The center's interior is uniformly finished in a cream color, and the terrazzo floor uses coloring and patterns harmonizing with the interior finish. The decorated lighting appliances, clocks, handrails, etc. are finished in the old green Victorian style. Within the commercial territory of this facility, there are about 1.5 million inhabitants, so these use two parking lots — one for 1,290 cars on the upper mall level (two floors) and on the roof, and the other for 220 cars in the basement of the leisure center.

● THE GLADES
Address: High Street Bromley, UK
Opened: October 22, 1991
Developer: Capital & Counties Plc
Design: Chapman Taylor Partners
Area: 30,000 m²
Number of cars parked: 1,510
Key tenants: Boots, Debenhams, Marks & Spencer, Littlewoods
Number of tenants: 135

ブロムレイ（Bromley）はロンドンの東南 約18キロにある人口30万人の町。〈ザ グレーズ＝THE GLADES〉は 市の中心部 約45,000㎡を 総合開発しオープンしたもので 住宅（ユニット） 教会 レジャーセンターを併設している。Upper mall level と Lower mall level の2層で 〈Boots〉 〈Debenhams〉 〈Marks & Spencer〉 〈Littlewoods〉 を核テナントとし 合計135店舗で構成。Lower mall level の "リージェントアーケード（Regent arcade）" には それぞれスタイルの違う6つのファストフード店 と 330席のフードコートが設けられ人気を集めている。センター内は淡いクリーム色で統一され テラゾーの床もそれに調和した色彩とパターンが使用されている。また デコレイトされた照明や時計 手摺などはグリーンのオールド ビクトリアン スタイルでまとめられている。商圏内には 約150万人が住み その集客ポイントとしてモールの上層階（2層分）と屋上に1,290台 レジャーセンターの地下に220台のパーキングスペースを確保している。

●ザ グレーズ
住所：   High Street Bromley, UK
開店：   1991年10月22日
デベロッパー： Capital & Counties Plc
設計：   Chapman Taylor Partners
面積：   30,000㎡
駐車台数：   1,510
キーテナント： Boots, Debenhams, Marks & Spencer, Littlewoods
テナント数：   135

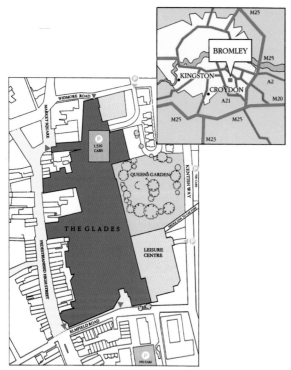

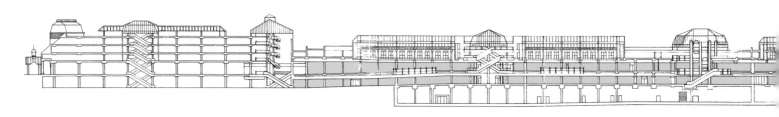

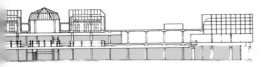

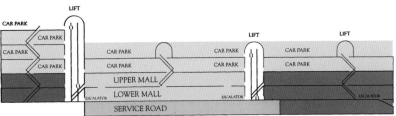

UPPER MALL LEVEL

LOWER MALL LEVEL

PRINCES QUAY

〈Kingston Upon Hull, UK〉

"PRINCES QUAY" opened in March 1992 by redeveloping a dock at Kingston Upon Hull which became unnecessary as a result of decline of the shipping business. At the time of redevelopment, since sludge 4 m in depth had accumulated on the ground which is clay and sand to a depth of 15 m, stakes were driven into the ground so that the building sits on them. The length of stakes used totaled 30 m, next only to 35 m — the longest application example in the U.K. With an atrium in the center, the glazed building has 3 levels. The double airtight system protects the building from the direct heat of the sun, preventing the inside temperature from rising. The basement is a floor of restaurants offering light meals with a food court that descends in steps to the water's edge.

The mall is tenanted by a total of 91 shops, centering around "Allders," the "Bunptons Group," "Sears" and "Spoils." By installing an approach from the entrance which gives the image of a deck, and also approaches extending in an X shape from the atrium, the interior layout is spacious and bright, and comfortably composed.

● PRINCES QUAY

Address:	Princes Dock Kingston Upon Hull, UK
Opened:	March 1992
Developer:	Land Securities plc, BICC Developments Ltd., Teesland Development Co., Ltd.
Design:	Hugh Martin Partnership
Area:	26,300 m²
Number of cars parked:	1,000
Key tenants:	Allders, Buptons Group, Sears, Spoils
Number of tenants:	91

〈プリンセス キー＝PRINCES QUAY〉は 海運の斜陽化で不要になったキングストーン アポン フルのドックを再開発し 1992年3月にオープンした。当時ドックは 4メートルの沈泥が蓄積されており さらにその下の地盤は15メートルの深さにわたり粘土質と砂地であるため クイを打ち込み 建物はその上に乗っかったスタイルになっている。使用されたクイは30メートルにも及び 英国では最長の35メートルに次ぐ長さのものになった。ガラス張りで中央部にアトリウムを持つ建物は3層で 二重密封システムを採用することで 太陽の直射熱をさけ 内部の温度上昇を防いでいる。地階はリフレッシュメント(軽食レストラン)のフロアで 水辺にステップダウンさせたフードコートが設けられている。

モールは〈Allders〉〈Buptons Group〉〈Sears〉〈Spoils〉を核に 合計91店のテナントで構成。エントランスからのデッキをイメージさせるアプローチや アトリウムからX字状に延びたアプローチなど 余裕をもたせた館内は明るく 快適な空間構成がなされている。

● プリンセス キー

住所：	Princes Dock Kingston Upon Hull, UK
開店：	1992年3月
デベロッパー：	Land Securities plc, BICC Developments Ltd., Teesland Development Co.,Ltd.
設計：	Hugh Martin Partnership
面積：	26,300㎡
駐車台数：	1,000
キーテナント：	Allders, Buptons Group, Sears, Spoils
テナント数：	91

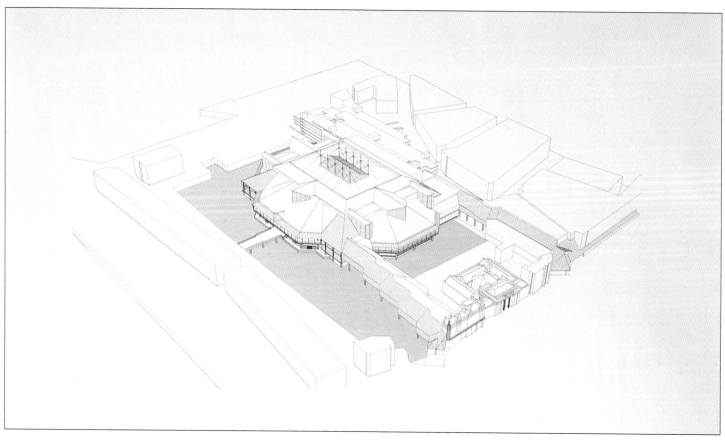

FACILITIES

KEY

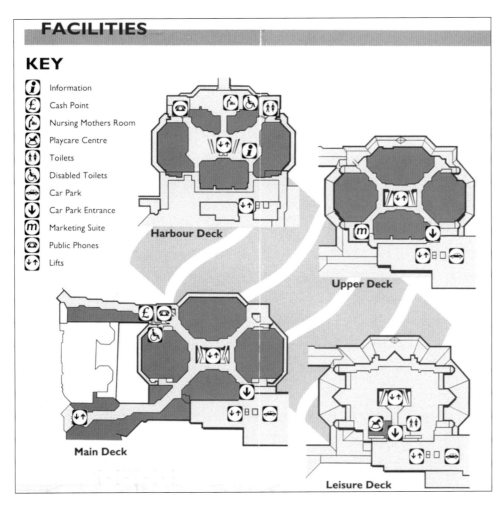

- ⓘ Information
- £ Cash Point
- Nursing Mothers Room
- Playcare Centre
- Toilets
- Disabled Toilets
- Car Park
- Car Park Entrance
- ⓜ Marketing Suite
- Public Phones
- Lifts

Harbour Deck

Upper Deck

Main Deck

Leisure Deck

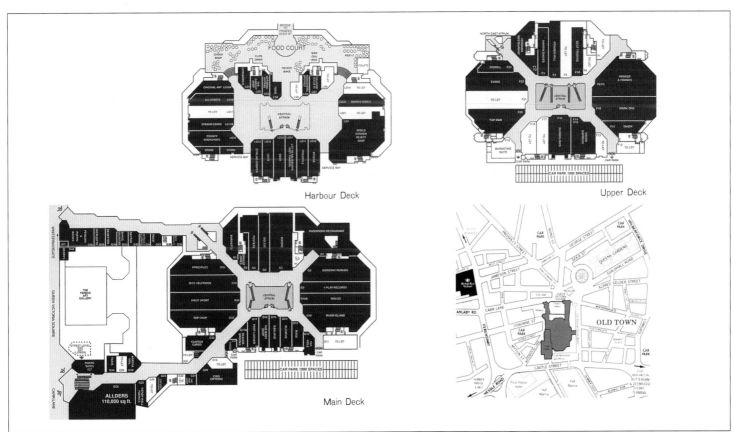

Harbour Deck

Upper Deck

Main Deck

LOS ARCOS

〈Sevilla, Spain〉

"LOS ARCOS" was constructed as part of the general redevelopment of a residential quarter with an area of 25,250 m² on the eastern side of Sevilla City. It opened in October 1992 when the Sevilla Expo ended. As a result of competition between architects and designers in Sevilla, the "traditional architectural style in Sevilla, combined with simpleness and modernity," was finally adopted as the design concept of this facility.

Arch, tower, pargola, terra-cotta, ceramic, glass, etc. — elements or methods typical of the Sevilla style — were adopted, while the facade is finished with colored concrete blocks, thus creating a fresh image. The building has 3 levels each with a parking area, accommodating 1,800 cars in total. "Planta baja" (on the 1st floor) consists of shops dealing in goods for daily life, fashion goods, etc. "Planta alta" (on the 2nd floor) has a home furnishings corner, a restaurant, etc. "Planta terraza" (on the highest floor) is tenanted by 145 shops including a movie theater, leisure activity facilities and restaurants. Along with other facilities, the movie theater, which has 12 screens, is gaining popularity.

● LOS ARCOS
Address: Avenida de Andalucia,
                     Ronda del Tamarguillo E-Sevilla, Spain
Opened: October 1992
Developer: Inmobiliaria Norte Sur, S.A.
Design: Equipo Naib-Sevilla, Design International-London
Area: 43,300 m²
Number of cars parked: 1,800
Key tenants: PRYCA, TOYS 'R' US, C & A
Number of tenants: 145

〈ロス アルコス＝LOS ARCOS〉は セビーリャ市の中心から東側の居住区域 25,250㎡ の 総合再開発の一環として建設されたもので セビーリャ万博（Sevilla Expo）が終わった 1992年10月にオープンした。設計はセビーリャの建築家やデザイナーによるコンペで "セビーリャの伝統的な建築様式のなかにシンプルさとモダン性をもたせたもの" をデザインコンセプトに決定された。アーチ タワー パーゴラ テラコッタ セラミック ガラスなど典型的なセビーリャ スタイルと手法が採り入れられ ファサードは カラーコンクリート ブロック積みで仕上げられ 革新的である。建物は 3層で各階にそれぞれパーキングスペースがあり トータルで1,800台が収容できる。1階 "Planta baja" は 生活用品とファッション スクエアーなど 2階 "Planta alta" は ホームファニシングとレストラン 最上階 "Planta terraza" は 映画館 レジャーアクティビティ レストランなど 145店のテナントミックスで 特に12基のスクリーンを持つ映画館は人気を博している。

● ロス アルコス
住所：   Avenida de Andalucia, Ronda del Tamarguillo E-Sevilla, Spain
開店：   1992年10月
デベロッパー： Inmobiliaria Norte Sur, S.A.
設計：   Equipo Naib-Sevilla, Design International-London
面積：   43,300㎡
駐車台数：   1,800
キーテナント： PRYCA, TOYS 'Я'US, C & A
テナント数：   145

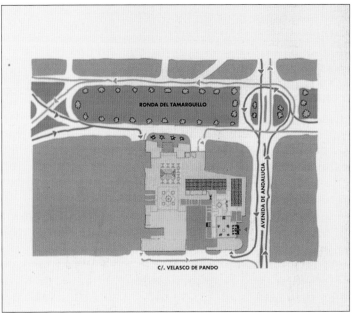

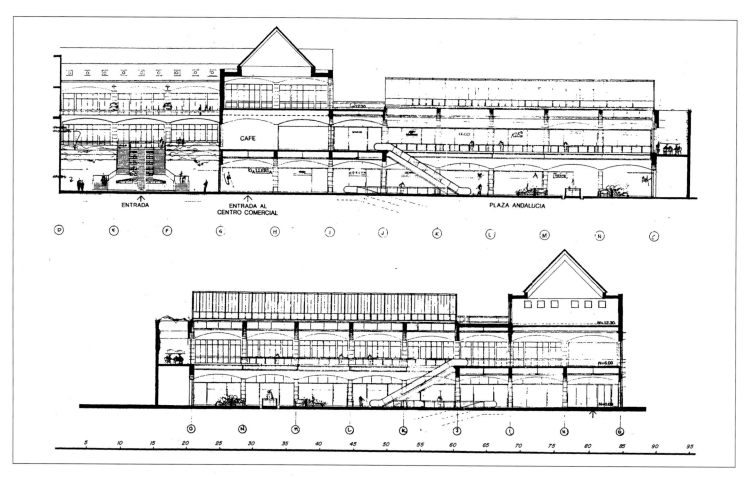

ENTRADA

ENTRADA AL
CENTRO COMERCIAL

PLAZA ANDALUCIA

CAFE

GALLERIA

N+12.30

N+6.00

N+0.00

5 10 15 20 25 30 35 40 45 50 55 60 65 70 75 80 85 90 95

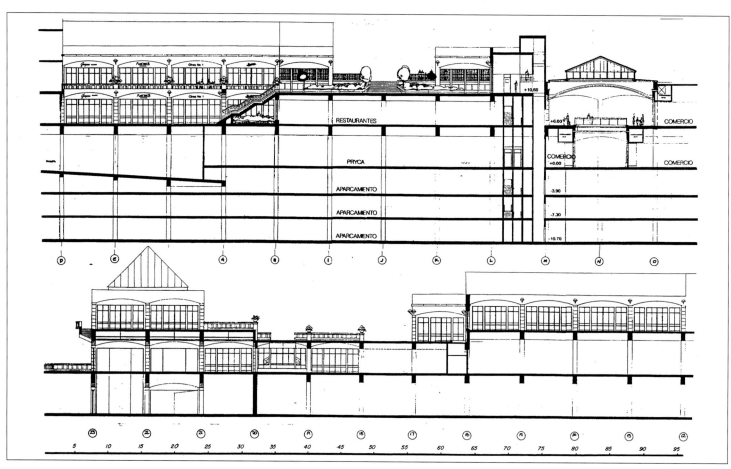

RESTAURANTES

PRYCA

APARCAMENTO

APARCAMENTO

APARCAMENTO

+10.60

+6.00

COMERCIO
+0.00

-3.90

-7.30

-10.70

COMERCIO

COMERCIO

COMERCIO

5 10 15 20 25 30 35 40 45 50 55 60 65 70 75 80 85 90 95

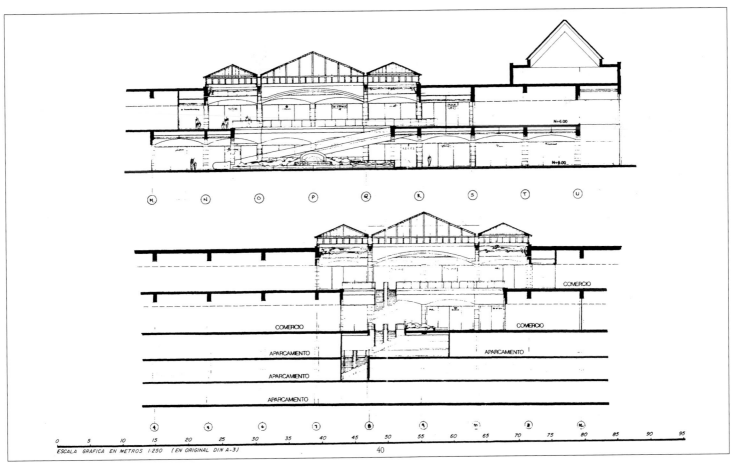

ESCALA GRAFICA EN METROS 1:250 (EN ORIGINAL DIN A-3)

40

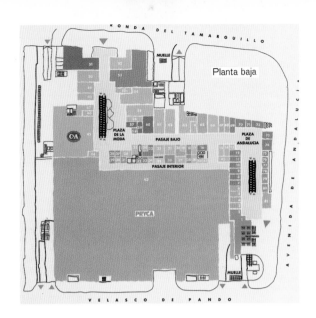

Planta baja

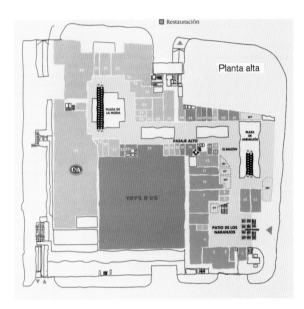

□ Restauración

Planta alta

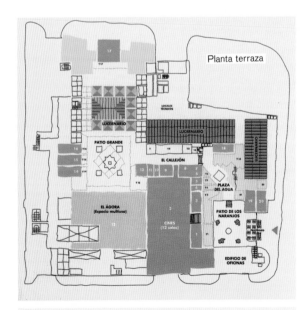

Planta terraza

□ Vestido y calzado
□ Alimentación especializada
□ Otros comparativos
□ Servicios
■ Equipamientos del hogar
□ Otros cotidianos
■ Restauración

SLOTS ARKADERNE

⟨Hillerød, Denmark⟩

Situated on an old street leading to the Castle Frederiksborg in Hillerød City about 35 km north of Copenhagen. Development of this shopping center was subjected to various restrictions by the municipal authorities: perfect preservation of the existing street features without any changes in width, etc., and harmony of the building height, roof, etc. with the surrounding environment. "SLOTS ARKADERNE" is composed of three sections, and Nordstensuej Street which runs through the facility, can be crossed through a tunnel. Each section features blue metallic framework and is provided with an atrium designed in the image of the royal crown. These sections are joined by an arcade. The atrium space comes with crown-shaped chandeliers varying in size which serve as a symbol of the shopping center. Residences and a library are also adjacent to the center. Thus, due to an environment that is convenient for the neighboring inhabitants and shoppers, the center is operating successfully.

●SLOTS ARKADERNE

Address: Slots Arkaderne DK-3400 Hillerød, Denmark
Opened: October 1992
Developer: Danica Investments, Højgaad & Schultz
Design: Plesner & Wajnman/Arkitektkontoret of 1983
Area: 29,600 m²
Number of cars parked: 1,100
Key tenants: OBS
Number of tenants: 50

コペンハーゲンの北 約35キロ ヒレロット (Hillerød) の Frederiksborg 城に通じる 旧市街地に立地している。開発にあたっては市当局から 現存する通りの特徴を完全に保ち 条件や幅など変更しないこと 建物の高さや屋根など周囲の環境に調和させること などの制約を受けている。
 〈スロッツ アーケードヌ＝SLOTS ARKADERNE〉は 3つのセクションで構成され 施設内を走る Nordstensuej 通りは地下道で横断できる。各々のセクションにはブルーのメタリックの骨組みで王室のクラウンをイメージしたアトリウムが設けられ アーケードでジョイントしている。アトリウムには クラウン形の大小のシャンデリアが下げられシンボル的な存在になっている。 このセンターには住宅や図書館も併設されており住人や買い物客に対し利用しやすい環境づくりで成功をおさめている。

●スロッツ アーケードヌ

住所：   Slots Arkaderne DK-3400 Hillerød, Denmark
開店：   1992年10月
デベロッパー：Danica Investments, Højgaad & Schultz
設計：   Plesner & Wajnman/Arkitektkontoret of 1983
面積：   29,600㎡
駐車台数：   1,100
キーテナント：OBS
テナント数：   50

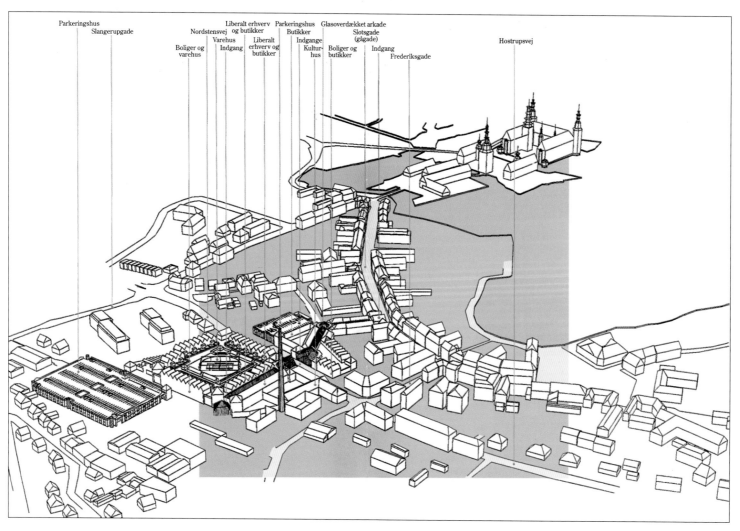

Parkeringshus
Slangerupgade
Boliger og
varehus
Nordstensvej
Varehus
Indgang
Liberalt
erhverv og
butikker
Liberalt erhverv
og butikker
Parkeringshus
Butikker
Indgange
Kultur-
hus
Glasoverdækket arkade
Slotsgade
(gågade)
Boliger og
butikker
Indgang
Frederiksgade
Hostrupsvej

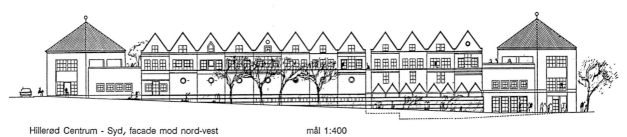

Hillerød Centrum - Syd, facade mod nord-vest   mål 1:400

Hillerød Centrum - Syd, facade mod syd-vest   mål 1:400

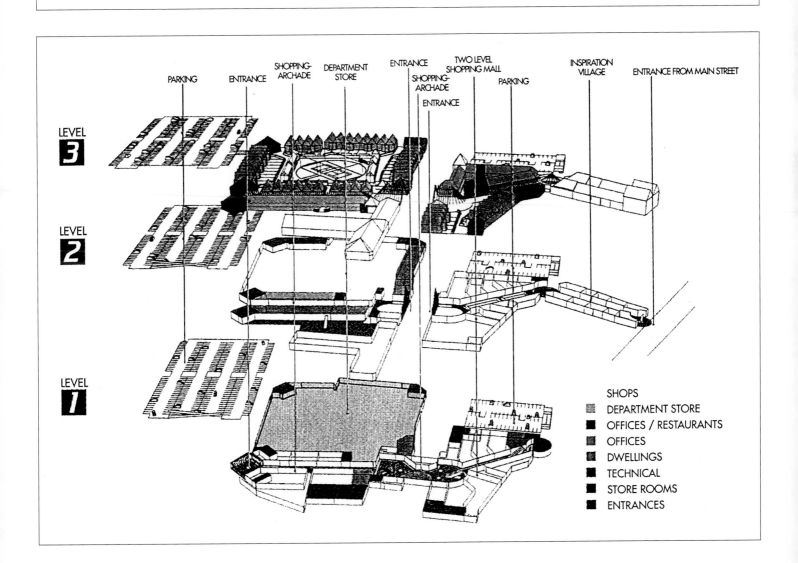

PARKING   ENTRANCE   SHOPPING-   DEPARTMENT   ENTRANCE   TWO LEVEL   INSPIRATION   ENTRANCE FROM MAIN STREET
                         ARCHADE   STORE   SHOPPING MALL VILLAGE
                                                     SHOPPING-   PARKING
                                                     ARCHADE
                                                     ENTRANCE

LEVEL
3

LEVEL
2

LEVEL
1

SHOPS
DEPARTMENT STORE
OFFICES / RESTAURANTS
OFFICES
DWELLINGS
TECHNICAL
STORE ROOMS
ENTRANCES

HEUVEL GALERIE

⟨Eindhoven, Netherlands⟩

The "HEUVEL GALERIE" opened in conjunction with the redevelopment of the central part of Eindhoven in the southeastern area of the Netherlands. It is one of the Netherlands' largest facilities, covering a total area of 60,000 m², with the shopping center (26,000 m²) and culture center mixed. The interior space is composed of shops, a casino, a music center (with 1,200 seats), offices, flats (44 residences), an underground parking lot (accommodating 1,160 cars), etc.

The mall is 220 m in total length, and is tenanted by 115 shops. The entrance hall and arcade are decorated with ceiling paintings and also objects such as sculptures here and there. In the domed atrium called the "Forum," live music is performed at lunchtime and in the evening. The staircase area is also used as a fashion show stage. A hundred years ago, Eindhoven was an agricultural town having a population of only 5,000. However, during this century, its population has increased to about 200,000 and the city has developed into an industrial center, as the capital of the Brabant District. As the new city center, if not as a shopping center, this facility is utilized not merely by community inhabitants but also by people from other cities and by foreigners.

● HEUVEL GALERIE

Address: Heuvel Galerie 133 NL-5611 DK
                  Eindhoven, Netherlands
Opened: 1992
Developer: MAB B.V.
Design: Walter Brune architectur,
                  Aken B.V. Architectur & Stedebouw
Area: 26,000 m²
Number of cars parked: 1,160
Key tenants: Hennes & Mauritz, Intertoys,
                  Van Piere Boeken, De Jong
Number of tenants: 115

このⓇ〈ホイフェル ガレリー＝HEUVEL GALERIE〉はオランダの南東部 アイントホーフェン（Eindhoven）の中心部の再開発によりオープンした。ショッピングセンター（26,000㎡）とカルチャーセンターをミックスさせた総面積 60,000㎡に及ぶ オランダ最大規模の開発で 店舗　カジノ　ミュージックセンター（1200席）オフィス　フラット（住宅＝44軒）地下駐車場（1160台収容）等で構成されている。モールは全長220メートルで115店舗のテナントが出店している。エントランスホールやアーケードには天井画が描かれ 随所に彫刻などが置かれている。"Forum"と呼ばれるドームのアトリウムでは昼食時や夕方にはライブミュージックが演奏され 階段はファッションショーの舞台にも使用されている。100年前はわずか5000人の人口だった農業の町 アイントホーフェンも この1世紀の間に約20万人となり ブラバント地方（Brabant）の首都　工業都市へとして発展している。この施設はショッピングセンターというよりは 新しいシティセンターといった感覚で 住民のみでなく国内外の人々に利用されている。

●ホイフェル ガレリー

住所：　　　　　Heuvel Galerie 133 NL-5611 DK Eindhoven, Netherlands
開店：　　　　　1992年
デベロッパー：　MAB B.V
設計：　　　　　Walter Brune architectur, Aken B.V. Architectur & Stedebouw
面積：　　　　　26,000㎡
駐車台数：　　　1,160
キーテナント：　Hennes & Mauritz, Intertoys, Van Piere Boeken, De Jong
テナント数：　　115

6 woningen Nieuwstraat

38 woningen Ravensdonck

Multifunktioneel projekt Heuvelgalerie

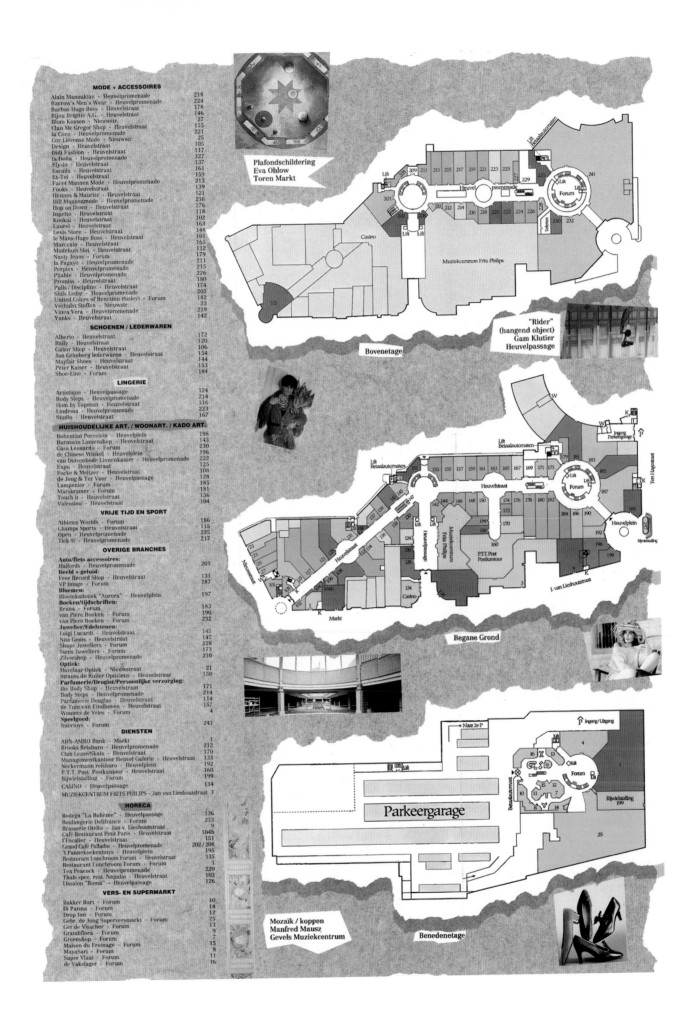

MODE + ACCESSOIRES

Alain Manoukian - Heuvelpromenade	218
Barrow's Men's Wear - Heuvelpromenade	224
Barbas Hugo Boss - Heuvelstraat	178
Bijou Brigitte A.G. - Heuvelstraat	146
Blom Kousen - Nieuwstr.	27
Clan Mc Gregor Shop - Heuvelstraat	155
la Coco - Heuvelpromenade	221
Cor Lievense Mode - Nieuwstr.	25
Design - Heuvelstraat	105
Didi Fashion - Heuvelstraat	117
la Doña - Heuvelpromenade	227
Elysio - Heuvelstraat	137
Escada - Heuvelstraat	161
Et-Tol - Heuvelstraat	159
Facet Mannen Mode - Heuvelpromenade	213
Fooks - Heuvelstraat	139
Hennes & Mauritz - Heuvelstraat	121
Hill Mannenmode - Heuvelpromenade	216
Hop on Down - Heuvelstraat	176
Inpetto - Heuvelstraat	118
Kookai - Heuvelstraat	102
Laurel - Heuvelstraat	163
Levis Store - Heuvelstraat	148
le Mans-Hugo Boss - Heuvelstraat	101
Marccain - Heuvelstraat	165
Modehuis Slot - Heuvelstraat	112
Nasty Jeans - Forum	179
la Pagayo - Heuvelpromenade	211
Perplex - Heuvelpromenade	215
Pliable - Heuvelpromenade	226
Promiss - Heuvelstraat	180
Pulls / Discipline - Heuvelstraat	174
Sluis Leder - Heuvelpromenade	205
United Colors of Benetton (Sisley) - Forum	182
Verhulst Stoffen - Nieuwstr.	23
Vinca Vera - Heuvelpromenade	219
Yanks - Heuvelstraat	142

SCHOENEN / LEDERWAREN

Alberto - Heuvelstraat	172
Bally - Heuvelstraat	120
Gabor Shop - Heuvelstraat	106
Jan Grimberg lederwaren - Heuvelstraat	154
Mayfair Shoes - Heuvelstraat	144
Peter Kaiser - Heuvelstraat	153
Shoe-Line - Forum	184

LINGERIE

Artistique - Heuvelpassage	124
Body Steps - Heuvelpromenade	214
Hom by Topman - Heuvelstraat	116
Lindessa - Heuvelpromenade	223
Studio - Heuvelstraat	167

HUISHOUDELIJKE ART. / WOONART. / KADO ART.

Bohemian Porcelein - Heuvelplein	198
Burmann Linnenshop - Heuvelstraat	143
Casa Leonardo - Forum	230
de Chinese Winkel - Heuvelplein	196
van Duivenbode Linnenkamer - Heuvelpromenade	222
Expo - Heuvelstraat	125
Focke & Meltzer - Heuvelstraat	108
de Jong & Ter Veer - Heuvelpassage	128
Lampenier - Forum	185
Marckramer - Forum	181
Touch it - Heuvelstraat	156
Valentino - Heuvelstraat	104

VRIJE TIJD EN SPORT

Athletes Worlds - Forum	186
Champs Sports - Heuvelstraat	115
Open - Heuvelpromenade	225
Tick-It - Heuvelpromenade	217

OVERIGE BRANCHES

Auto/fiets accessoires:
Halfords - Heuvelpromenade	201

Beeld + geluid:
Free Record Shop - Heuvelstraat	131
VP Image - Forum	187

Bloemen:
Bloemkadotiek "Aurora" - Heuvelplein	197

Boeken/tijdschriften:
Bruna - Forum	183
van Piere Boeken - Forum	190
van Piere Boeken - Forum	232

Juwelier/Edelstenen:
Luigi Lucardi - Heuvelstraat	145
Nita Gems - Heuvelstraat	147
Shape Juweliers - Forum	228
Stern Juweliers - Forum	173
Zilvershop - Heuvelpromenade	210

Optiek:
Havelaar Optiek - Nieuwstraat	21
Strauss.de Ruiter Opticiens - Heuvelstraat	150

Parfumerie/Drogist/Persoonlijke verzorging:
the Body Shop - Heuvelstraat	171
Body Steps - Heuvelpromenade	214
Parfumerie Douglas - Heuvelstraat	114
de Tuin van Eindhoven - Heuvelstraat	157
Wouters de Vries - Forum	4

Speelgoed:
Intertoys - Forum	241

DIENSTEN

ABN-AMRO Bank - Markt	1
Brooks Reisburo - Heuvelpromenade	212
Club Lease/Skala - Heuvelstraat	170
Managementkantoor Heuvel Galerie - Heuvelstraat	133
Neckermann reisburo - Heuvelplein	192
P.T.T. Post Postkantoor - Heuvelstraat	160
Rijwielstalling - Forum	199
CASINO - Heuvelpassage	134
MUZIEKCENTRUM FRITS PHILIPS - Jan van Lieshoutstraat	3

HORECA

Bodega "La Bohème" - Heuvelpassage	136
Boulangerie Delifrance - Forum	233
Brasserie Otello - Jan v. Lieshoutstraat	9
Café Restaurant Petit Paris - Heuvelstraat	104b
l'Escalier - Heuvelstraat	151
Grand Café Palladio - Heuvelpromenade	202 / 208
't Pannenkoekenhuys - Heuvelplein	195
Restaurant Lunchroom Forum - Heuvelstraat	135
Restaurant Lunchroom Forum - Forum	1
Tea Peacock - Heuvelpromenade	220
Thais spec. rest. Napalai - Heuvelstraat	103
IJssalon "Roma" - Heuvelpassage	126

VERS- EN SUPERMARKT

Bakker Bart - Forum	10
Di Parma - Forum	14
Drop Inn - Forum	12
Gebr. de Jong Superversmarkt - Forum	25
Ger de Visscher - Forum	13
Grandiflora - Forum	9
Greenshop - Forum	7
Maison du Fromage - Forum	15
MayaSari - Forum	8
Super Vlaai - Forum	11
de Vakslager - Forum	16

Plafondschildering
Eva Ohlow
Toren Markt

"Rider"
(hangend object)
Gam Klutier
Heuvelpassage

Bovenetage

Begane Grond

Benedenetage

Parkeergarage

Mozaïk / koppen
Manfred Mausz
Gevels Muziekcentrum

BAHIA SUR

⟨San Fernando (Càdiz), Spain⟩

Completed in San Fernando in the suburbs of the port town of Càdiz in the southern part of Spain on the Atlantic Ocean, "BAHIA SUR" is a general commercial/leisure center developed by Parques Urvanos within Càdiz Bay. Covering a huge area of 117,000 m², it is composed of a sports club, a hotel, bungalows, a disco, a shopping center, residences, etc.
The facade is in the Andalusian style and has a tower, and, to avoid the strong sunlight of the southern country, the shopping center is underground with tennis courts, a soccer stadium and other sports facilities above. Thus, it differs from ordinary style in which light is directly let in from the top light. There are two parking lots which can accommodate a total of 3,000 cars.
With "Pryca" (a hypermarket: 10,500 m²) and "Galerias Preciados" (a department store) as the key tenants, the shop space looks like an oasis, and is favorably accepted not merely by community inhabitants but also by resort visitors and tourists.

●BAHIA SUR
Address: GMR Asessores Caño Herrera s/n
E-11100 San Fernando (Càdiz), Spain
Opened: July 1992
Developer: Parques Urbanos S.A.
Design: Juan Thomas, Antonio Lòpez,
J. M. Lòpez, Lligia de Bernabé
Area: 56,000 m²
Number of cars parked: 3,000
Key tenants: Pryca, Galerias Preciados
Number of tenants: 175

大西洋に面するスペイン南部の港町 カディス(Càdiz)の近郊 サンフェルナンド(San Fernando)に完成した ⟨バヒア ソール＝BAHIA SUR⟩ は Parques Urvanos 社がカディス湾に開発した総合コマーシャル レジャーセンターで スポーツクラブ ホテル バンガロー ディスコ ショッピングセンター 住宅等で構成される 総面積 117,000㎡の広大なものである。建物の外観はタワーを有したアンダルシア地方の様式で ショッピングセンターは南国特有の強い直射光線を避けてテニスコートやサッカー場など スポーツ施設がある地下の部分に設けられ トップライトから直接採光する一般的な様式と異なっている。
駐車場は2ケ所で 合計で3000台が駐車可能。⟨Pryca⟩ (ハイパーマーケット＝10,500㎡)と⟨Galerias Preciados⟩(百貨店)をキーテナントにした オアシス的な余裕のある店舗構成は 地域住民はもとよりリゾート客やツーリストからも人気を得ている。

●バヒア ソール
住所： GMR Asessores Caño Herrera s/n E-11100 San Fernando (Càdiz), Spain
開店： 1992年 7月
デベロッパー： Parques Urbanos S.A.
設計： Juan Thomas, Antonio Lòpez, J.M.L pez, Lligia de Bernabé
面積： 56,000㎡
駐車台数： 3,000
キーテナント： Pryca, Galerias Preciados
テナント数： 175

KINGS WALK

⟨London, UK⟩

Chelsea is a place which may be said to be the birthplace of London fashion. "KINGS WALK" is a shopping mall opened about 500 m away from Sloan Square, where the Kings Road starts.

It has an area of about 3,000 m^2 and is composed of 22 tenant shops. It is drawing attention as a model of small-scale commercial facility development. The basic design emphasis is placed on the architectural balance between the upper and lower levels of the vertical atrium space. Two glazed see-through elevators with exposed metallic frames are installed on the right side of the entrance. On the opposite side from the central part, a suspension bridge is installed, behind which an escalator and staircase are placed. Thus, spatial balance is retained. Among other features the steel-made suspension bridge uses members resembling stretched piano wires. It is visually dynamic and buoyant, and also looks like a stage-passage at a fashion show. It is intended to produce a multiplying effect, linked with the flow of people.

● KINGS WALK

Address: 122 Kings Road Chelsea London, SW3 UK
Opened: November 1988
Developer: County and District Properties
Design: Crighton Mc Coll/ Damond Lock Grabrowski
Area: 3,000 m^2
Number of cars parked: 0
Key tenants: The Gap
Number of tenants: 22

チェルシー(Chelsea)地区は ロンドンファッション発祥の地である。 この〈キングス ウォーク＝KINGS WALK〉は その草分け的なストリート キングスロード(Kings Road)の始まるスローンスクエア(Sloan Square)から 約500メートルのところにオープンしたショッピングモール。総面積 約3,000㎡ 22店のテナントで構成 小規模な商業施設開発のモデルとして注目されている。アトリウムの上下 即ち垂直的な空間を いかに建築的に効率よく対応させるかを 基本コンセプトにデザインされている。エントランス方向から見て 右側にメタリックな骨格を露出させたガラス張りのシースルーエレベーターを 2基設置し その中心部から反対側につり橋を架設 その奥にエスカレーター 手前には階段を配し 空間でのバランスを保っている。特にピアノ線を張ったようなスティールのつり橋は ビジュアル的に跳躍感があり軽快で ファッションショーの花道のようでもあり 人の流れとの相乗効果をねらっている。

● キングス ウォーク

住所： 122 Kings Road Chelsea London, SW3 UK
開店： 1988年11月
デベロッパー：County and District Properties
設計： Crighton Mc Coll/Damond Lock Grabrowski
面積： 3,000㎡
駐車台数： 0
キーテナント：The Gap
テナント数： 22

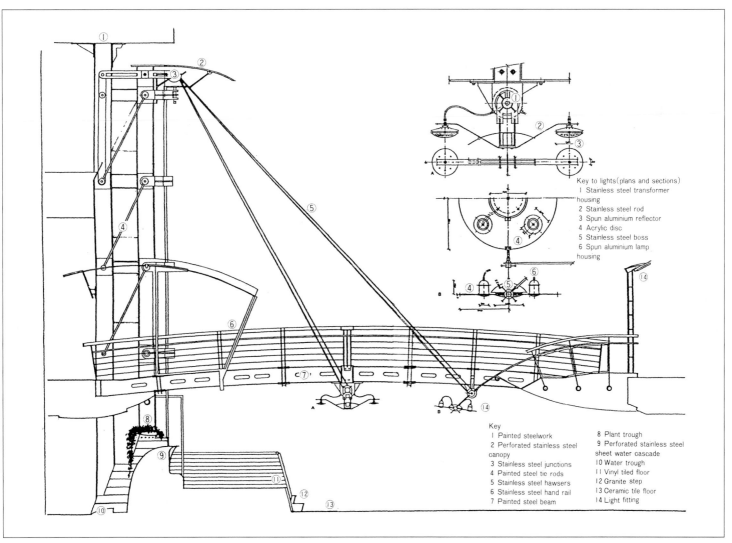

Key to lights(plans and sections)
1 Stainless steel transformer housing
2 Stainless steel rod
3 Spun aluminium reflector
4 Acrylic disc
5 Stainless steel boss
6 Spun aluminium lamp housing

Key
1 Painted steelwork
2 Perforated stainless steel canopy
3 Stainless steel junctions
4 Painted steel tie rods
5 Stainless steel hawsers
6 Stainless steel hand rail
7 Painted steel beam
8 Plant trough
9 Perforated stainless steel sheet water cascade
10 Water trough
11 Vinyl tiled floor
12 Granite step
13 Ceramic tile floor
14 Light fitting

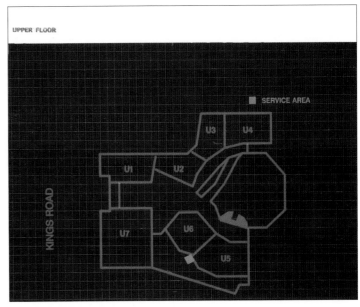

SERVICE AREA

KINGS ROAD

U3 U4

U1 U2

U7 U6

U5

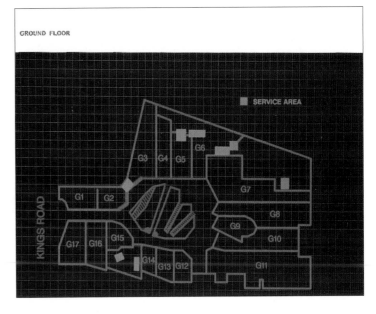

GROUND FLOOR

SERVICE AREA

G3 G4 G5 G6

G7

G1 G2

G8

G9

G17 G16 G15

G10

KINGS ROAD

G14 G13 G12

G11

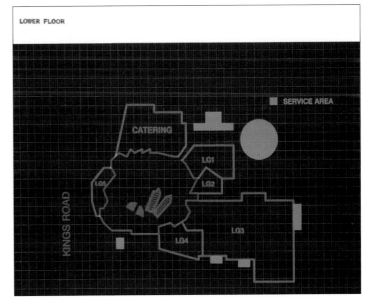

LOWER FLOOR

SERVICE AREA

CATERING

LG1

LG5

LG2

KINGS ROAD

LG4 LG3

LES TROIS QUARTIERS

⟨Paris, France⟩

"LES TROIS QUARTIERS," situated in front of La Madeleine in Paris, represents a renewal of the antiquated department store "Aux Trois Quartier" which was constructed in the 1930s. The new store opened in the fall of 1991. The architectural design was undertaken by Jean Jacques Ory, an architect, and the interior design, by Jean Michel Wilmotte.

It is connected by a tunnel to the subway station Porte Madeleine. The building retains the original image (a deluxe liner) of the time when it was first constructed. In view of the harmony with the surrounding environment, part of the exterior wall has been preserved to form the facade, thus succeeding in finishing the shopping space in a dignified style.

The selling area is 9,000 m² and composed of 70 selected tenant shops including fashion boutiques, beauty parlors and restaurants. An escalator is located in the central part. Benches are placed along the spacious aisle, thus creating the atmosphere of a liner's deck. The mall, with prestigious specialty shops, is drawing the attention of many people.

● LES TROIS QUARTIERS

Address: 23 boulevard de la Madeleine 75001 Paris, France
Opened: October 1991
Owner: Meiji Mutual Life Insurance Company), Postel Investment Management Ltd.
Design: Jean Jacques Ory, Jean Michel Wilmotte
Area: 9,000 m²
Number of cars parked: 0
Key tenants: Madelios Monsieur, Madelios Madame, Silver Moon, Restaurant Les Trois Quartiers
Number of tenants: 70

パリのマドレーヌ寺院(La Madeleine) の前に位置する ⟨レ トロワ カルティエ＝LES TROIS QUARTIERS⟩ は 1930年代に建造された百貨店 ⟨Aux Trois Quartier⟩ の老朽化によるリニューアルで 1991年秋にオープンした。 設計は建築家ジャン ジャック オリ(Jean Jacques Ory) と内装のジャン ミッシェル ヴィルモット(Jean Michel Wilmotte)。

メトロのマドレーヌ駅(Porte Madeleine) とは地下で接続されている。建物は建造当時のまま 豪華客船のイメージでまとめられ 周辺との調和を考慮し 外壁の一部をファサードに残した 格調高いショッピングスペースに仕上げている。売り場面積は9,000㎡でファッションブティック 美容室 レストランなど セレクトされた70店のテナントで構成。

中央部にはエスカレーターが設置されている。ゆったりと余裕を持たせた通路にはベンチが置かれ 客船のデッキの雰囲気である。プレステージの高い専門店を集めたこのモールは各方面から注目されている。

●レ トロワ カルティエ

住所：   23 boulevard de la Madeleine 75001 Paris, France
開店：   1991年10月
オーナー：   明治生命(Meiji Mutual Life Insurance Company), Postel Investment Management Ltd.
設計：   Jean Jacques Ory, Jean Michel Wilmotte
面積：   9,000㎡
駐車台数：   0
キーテナント：Madelios Monsieur, Madelios Madame, Silver Moon, Restaurant Les Trois Quartiers
テナント数：   70

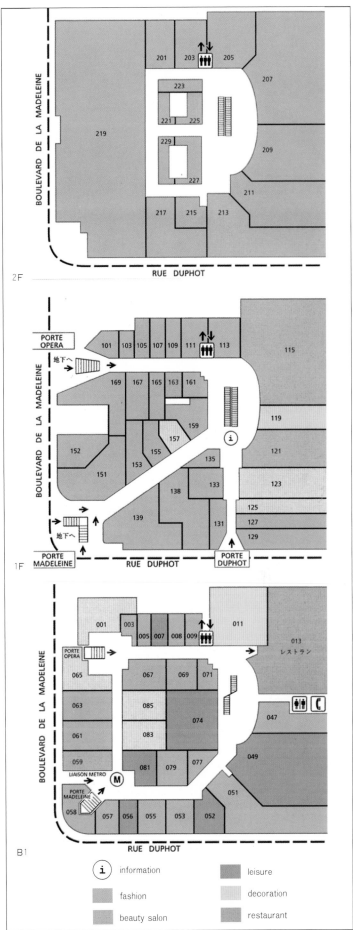

2F

1F

B1

i information

fashion

beauty salon

leisure

decoration

restaurant

BOULEVARD DE LA MADELEINE

RUE DUPHOT

PORTE OPERA

PORTE MADELEINE

PORTE DUPHOT

LIAISON METRO

ESPACE DROUET D'ERLON

⟨Reims, France⟩

Reims, in the northeastern part of France, is known for champagne vinting, and also as an important traffic point about 2 hours by train from Paris, Brussels, Luxemburg, etc. "ESPACE DROUET D'ERLON" is situated where the Place Drouet d'Erlon and Rue Buirette, which retain some medieval vestiges, cross. This relatively small mall (total selling space: 4,565 m²) is composed of 37 tenant shops including FNAC, the largest home electrical appliances and photographic ware dealer, which is developing its chain throughout France. Columns and marble are heavily used, and an atrium is located in the center. Different from ordinary urban shopping centers where importance is attached to the introduction of natural light from an atrium, this facility generally avoids natural light and introduces it only partially from an area which was formerly a courtyard. Instead, indirect light is cast on to the skyscape painted over the entire round ceiling, thus giving expanse to the interior space. Near the entrance, part of the medieval building is retained as the facade so that it stands in sharp contrast with the modern shopping space. Here, one can feel the continuity of the historical space through the modern architecture, as viewed by European architects.

● ESPACE DROUET D'ERLON

Address:　　　　　　53 Place d'Erlon 51100 Reims, France
Opened:　　　　　　June 4, 1992
Developer:　　　　　GEREC
Design:　　　　　　 Thienot-Ballan
Area:　　　　　　　 4,565 m²
Number of cars parked:　490
Key tenants:　　　　 FNAC
Number of tenants:　 37

フランス北東部のランス（Reims）は シャンペンの生産地として知られ パリ ブリュッセル ルクセンブルグなどから列車で2時間余りの交通の要所でもある。

〈エスパス ドロエ デロン＝ESPACE DROUET D'ERLON〉は 中世の面影を残す Place Drouet d'Erlon と Rue Buirette が交差する場所に位置している。総売場面積4,565㎡の比較的小規模なモールは フランス全国にチェーン展開する 家電と写真用品の最大大手〈FNAC〉をアンカーに合計37店のテナントで構成されている。円柱（コロン）と大理石を多用し 中央部にはアトリウムを設けている。都市型のショッピングセンターではアトリウムからの自然採光が重要視されているが ここでは開発にあたって裏庭だった部分から 一部分採光しているだけで意識的に避け 円形天井一面に大空を描き 間接光をあて 空間に拡がりを演出している。エントランス近くには 中世の建物の一部がファサードとして残され 近代的なショップ空間と対比させている。そこにはヨーロッパの建築家が抱いている 歴史空間の現代建築に対する継続性を感じることができる。

● エスパス ドロエ デロン

住所：　　　　　　　53 Place d'Erlon　51100 Reims, France
開店：　　　　　　　1992年6月4日
デベロッパー：　　　GEREC
設計：　　　　　　　Thienot-Ballan
面積：　　　　　　　4,565㎡
駐車台数：　　　　　490
キーテナント：FNAC
テナント数：　37

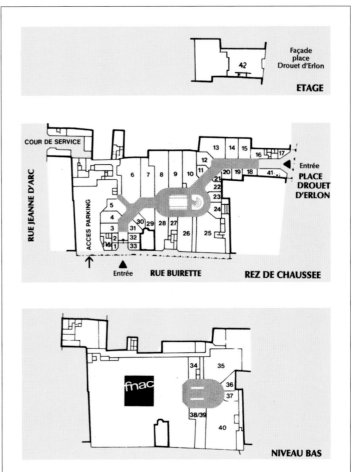

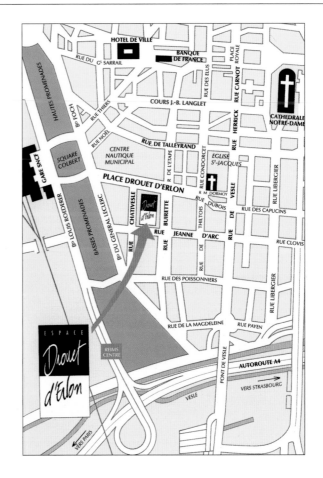

LILLE GRAND'PLACE

⟨Lille, France⟩

In the autumn of 1993, T.G.V. (the French national railways' bullet trains) opened in Lille in North France near the Belgian border. As a result, the time required for travelling between Lille and Paris has dramatically shortened to 1 hour and 20 minutes. "LILLE GRAND' PLACE" faces the Place du Géneral de Gaulle in the center of the city. As part of a general urban development project, the building of "La Voix du Nord" (a time-honored newspaper company in North France with a circulation of 400,000) has been renovated. It occupies the 1st floor of a building constructed by joining the existing commercial facilities (FNAC and Les Tanneurs) with the arched roofing which face each other across a road. The 2nd and higher floors of this building are used as offices. Although it is small in size (2,500 m²), it is composed of 14 high quality tenant shops including "Temerit" (men's wear), "Du Bon Cotê" (baby ware), and the Canadian brand "Yogen Früz" (cafe and fast food).

● LILLE GRAND' PLACE

Address:	Place du Géneral de Gaull 59000 Lille, France
Opened:	October 1992
Developer:	SCI Lille Grand' Place, ARC Union, Espace Promotion
Design:	Pierre Louis Carnèr
Area:	2,500 m²
Number of cars parked:	0
Key tenants:	FNAC
Number of tenants:	14

北フランスのベルギー国境沿いのリール (Lille) は 1993年秋にフランス国鉄高速列車 (TGV) が開通し リール～パリ間の所要時間は 1時間20分と これまでより大幅に短縮され便利になった。

⟨リール グラン プラス＝LILLE GRAND'PLACE⟩は市の中心部 ドゴール広場 (Place du Géneral de Gaulle) に面して立地している。総合市街地開発の一環として 新聞社 ("La Voix du Nord"北フランスの地方紙で 40万部の発行部数を誇り歴史のある) の社屋をリニューアルしオープンしたもの。道路を挟んで位置する既存の商業施設 (FNAC と Les Tanneurs) を アーチ型の屋根をかけてジョイントした 建物の1階部分で 2階以上はオフィスになっている。2,500㎡と小規模ではあるが ⟨Temerit⟩ (メンズ) ⟨Du Bon Cotê⟩ (ベビー用品) カナダブランドの ⟨Yogen Früz⟩ (カフェ＆ファスト フード) など クオリティの高い14店のテナントで構成されている。

● リール グラン プラス

住所：	Place du Géneral de Gaull 59000 Lille, France
開店：	1992年10月
デベロッパー：	SCI Lille Grand' Place, ARC Union, Espace Promotion
設計：	Pierre Louis Carnèr
面積：	2,500㎡
駐車台数：	0
キーテナント：	FNAC
テナント数：	14

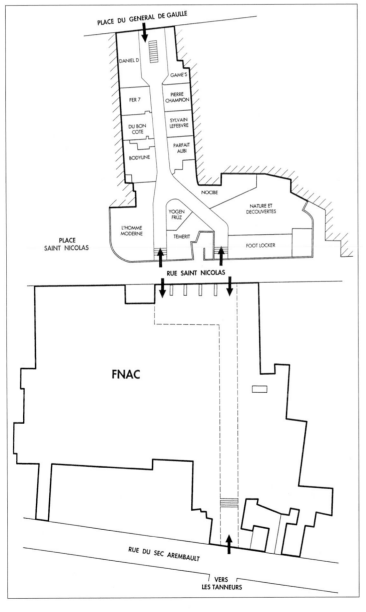

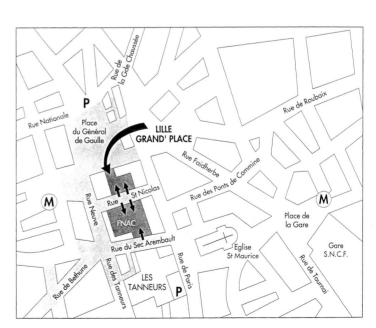

VICTORIA ISLAND

⟨London, UK⟩

Victoria Station, in the West End, constructed in the 18th century is the largest terminal station connecting London and the south-eastern parts of England. It is crowded with 200,000 passengers getting on and off everyday. Recently, it has become a terminal of the Airport Express, which connects the station with Gatwick Airport.

The station yard is divided into two parts one of which is included in the list of "Grade II" ranked historical buildings. "VICTORIA ISLAND" is a new complex created by removing the walls of both spaces. It is designed in the Victorian style and features a steel-framed arched ceiling with a glazed toplight. Since it uses slender pillars and a large glazed surface, it looks transparent and bright, and gives the image of an island which has appeared within the yard. The largest tenant is W. H. Smith, the largest book shop chain in England, which occupies the yard level and about half the total tenanted area on the 1st floor. The facility is also tenanted by take-out shops, tie shops, pubs, light meal restaurants, etc. for the convenience of tourists, businessmen on business trips, etc.

● VICTORIA ISLAND

Address: Victoria Station London SW1, UK
Opened: November 1992
Developer: British Rail Property Board
Design: Mc Coll
Area: 2,500 m²
Number of cars parked: 0
Key tenants: W. H. Smith
Number of tenants: 65

ウエスト エンド（West End）のヴィクトリア駅は18世紀に建造され ロンドンとイギリス東南部を結ぶ最大のターミナル駅であり 1日20万人の乗降客でにぎわう。最近ではガトウィック空港（Gatwick airport）と結ぶエアポートエキスプレスのターミナルにもなっている。構内は2つのパートに分かれており その一方は歴史的建造物のグレードⅡランクにリストアップされている。その両空間の壁を取り除いてつくられた新しいコンプレックスがこの〈ヴィクトリア アイランド＝VICTORIA ISLAND〉。フォルムはヴィクトリア様式をイメージしたデザインで その特徴である屋根にガラスのトップライトを持つ鉄骨のアーチ型。細い柱と 大きなサイズのガラス張りなので 透明感があり明るく 構内に出現した島といった感がある。テナントは イギリス最大のブックショップチェーンのW.H.Smith 社が 構内レベル（Concorce）と1階の総テナント面積の約半分を占め その他 テークアウト ネクタイショップ パブ 軽食レストランなど旅行者や出張者に便利な店舗構成になっている。

● ヴィクトリア アイランド

住所：   Victoria Station London SW1, UK
開店：   1992年11月
デベロッパー： British Rail Property Board
設計：   Mc Coll
面積：   2,500㎡
駐車台数：   0
キーテナント： W.H.Smith
テナント数：   65

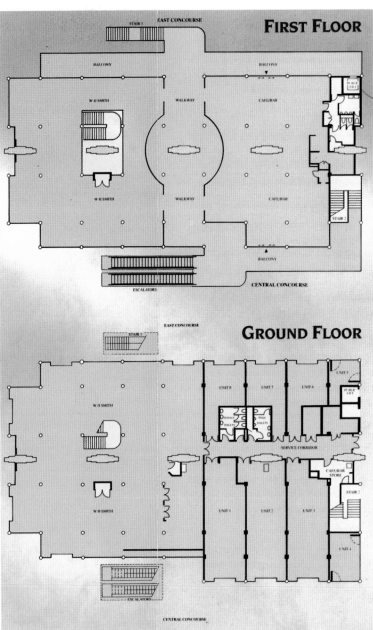

FIRST FLOOR

EAST CONCOURSE

STAIR 1

BALCONY

BALCONY

W H SMITH

WALKWAY

CAFE/BAR

W H SMITH

WALKWAY

CAFE/BAR

STAIR 2

BALCONY

ESCALATORS

CENTRAL CONCOURSE

GROUND FLOOR

EAST CONCOURSE

STAIR 1

W H SMITH

UNIT 8

UNIT 7

UNIT 6

UNIT 5

PUBLIC LIFT

FEMALE TOILETS

MALE TOILETS

SERVICE CORRIDOR

CAFE/BAR STORE

W H SMITH

UNIT 1

UNIT 2

UNIT 3

STAIR 2

UNIT 4

ESCALATORS

CENTRAL CONCOURSE

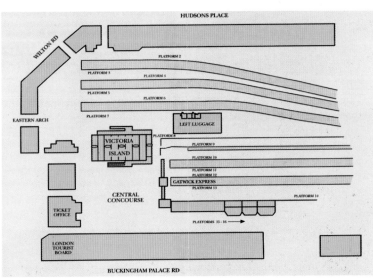

HUDSONS PLACE

WILTON RD

PLATFORM 2

PLATFORM 3

PLATFORM 4

PLATFORM 5

PLATFORM 6

EASTERN ARCH

PLATFORM 7

LEFT LUGGAGE

PLATFORM 8

VICTORIA ISLAND

PLATFORM 9

PLATFORM 10

PLATFORM 11

PLATFORM 12

GATWICK EXPRESS

PLATFORM 13

CENTRAL CONCOURSE

PLATFORM 14

TICKET OFFICE

PLATFORMS 15 - 16 →

LONDON TOURIST BOARD

BUCKINGHAM PALACE RD

EURALILLE

〈Lille, France〉

Lille City in North France is drawing attention as a center of the European traffic network, mainly due to the opening of T.G.V. (the French national railways' bullet trains) and the expected opening of the Channel Tunnel in 1994. Now, as the 21st century approaches, a new urban development project is underway by utilizing the advantageous features of this location.

"EURALILLE" is being constructed as part of the project for developing commercial and service facilities within a huge site extending from the conventional national railway station (Gare SNCF Lille-Frandres) and the T.G.V. station (Gare TGV Lille Europe whose building is under construction). It is a shopping center (70,000 m² in total floor area) centered round a mall. It is composed of three levels, including a mezzanine in one part. When completed, it will be tenanted by 150 shops centering around a hypermarket dealing mainly in foodstuffs. Ample space for restaurants, food centers, etc. is available and there is also a parking area capable of accommodating 2,900 cars. On the SNCF station side, 5 office buildings with 15 stories above ground are also being constructed. In addition, an office complex (55,000 m² in total area), including the World Trade Center and a 4-star hotel, is being constructed, with an expected completion date in the autumn of 1994. The facility design is being mainly undertaken by Jean Nouvel and Emmanuel Gattani. The structure uses a lot of metal frames and glass, and the roof is finished with alternately arranged opaque and transparent plates of glass. The facade is glazed in an open style, and is effectively accented with neon lamps which, when lit, bring a bright, comfortable commercial space into being, surrounded with dancing light. Around this facility, a conference hall (60,000 m²) and a park (15 hectares) are also being constructed. Thus, an urban space intended for the 21st century is being created rapidly.

フランス国鉄高速列車（TGV）の開通　チャンネル トンネルの開通（1994年予定）などでヨーロッパ交通網の中枢としてクローズアップされている北部フランスのリール市では　21世紀にむけて その地の利を活かした 新しい都市づくりの開発計画が進められている。

在来線の国鉄駅（Gare SNCF Lille-Flandres）と TGV駅（Gare TGV Lille Europe＝駅舎建設中）にまたがる広大な敷地内の　商業　サービス施設開発の一環として 建設中の〈ユーラリール＝EURALILLE〉は 総面積 70,000㎡のモールを主体にしたショッピングセンターで 2層 一部メザニン構造の 3層で構成され 完成時には食品をメインにしたハイパーマーケットを核に 150店のテナントが予定されている。レストランやフードセンターなどのスペースも充実され 地下には 2,900台収容可能の駐車スペースを設けている。SNCF駅側には地上15階建のオフィス棟が 5棟併設また コルビジェ通り（Rue le Dorbuiser）に面しては ワールドトレードセンターと4ツ星ホテルなど含む 55,000㎡のオフィスコンプレックスもそれぞれ1994年の秋の完成予定で建設中である。設計は Jean Nouvel と Emmanuel Gattani が核となっている。施設は メタルフレームとガラスを多用した構造で 屋根の部分には不透明と透明のガラスを交互に使用している。ファサードはガラス張りのオープン形式で ネオンが効果的に配され 点灯されると光が舞うような 明るい快適な商業空間の誕生となる。周囲には60,000㎡の会議場や15ヘクタールの公園も建設中で 環境を考慮した 21世紀を意識した都市空間造りが急ピッチで進められている。

●ユーラリール

住所：	Lille, France
開店：	1994年秋予定
デベロッパー：	Espace Promotion, SOPREC
設計：	Jean Nouvel, Emmanuel Gattani
面積：	70,000㎡
駐車台数：	2,900
テナント数：	150

●EURALILLE

Address:	Lille, France
Opened:	Autumn 1994 (planned)
Developer:	Espace Promotion, SOPREC
Design:	Jean Nouvel, Emmanuel Gattani
Area:	70,000 m²
Number of cars parked:	2,900
Number of tenants:	150

L'ARCHITECTURE

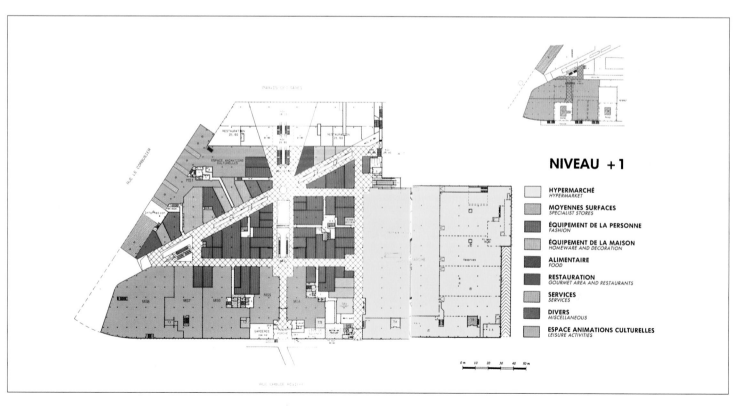

NIVEAU +1

- **HYPERMARCHÉ**
  HYPERMARKET
- **MOYENNES SURFACES**
  SPECIALIST STORES
- **ÉQUIPEMENT DE LA PERSONNE**
  FASHION
- **ÉQUIPEMENT DE LA MAISON**
  HOMEWARE AND DECORATION
- **ALIMENTAIRE**
  FOOD
- **RESTAURATION**
  GOURMET AREA AND RESTAURANTS
- **SERVICES**
  SERVICES
- **DIVERS**
  MISCELLANEOUS
- **ESPACE ANIMATIONS CULTURELLES**
  LEISURE ACTIVITIES

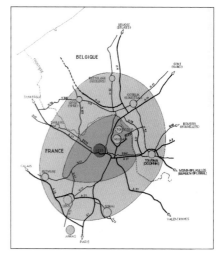

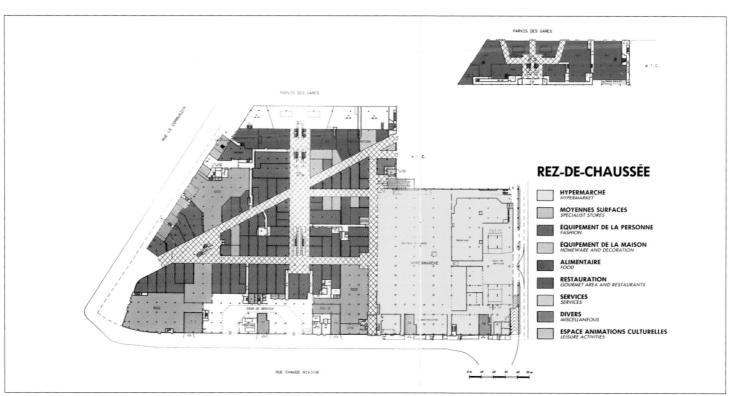

REZ-DE-CHAUSSÉE

- **HYPERMARCHÉ**
  HYPERMARKET
- **MOYENNES SURFACES**
  SPECIALIST STORES
- **ÉQUIPEMENT DE LA PERSONNE**
  FASHION
- **ÉQUIPEMENT DE LA MAISON**
  HOMEWARE AND DECORATION
- **ALIMENTAIRE**
  FOOD
- **RESTAURATION**
  GOURMET AREA AND RESTAURANTS
- **SERVICES**
  SERVICES
- **DIVERS**
  MISCELLANEOUS
- **ESPACE ANIMATIONS CULTURELLES**
  LEISURE ACTIVITIES

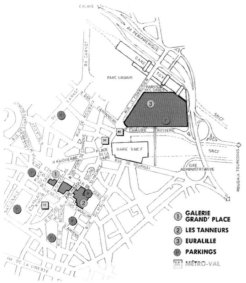

① GALERIE
GRAND' PLACE
② LES TANNEURS
③ EURALILLE
Ⓟ PARKINGS
Ⓜ MÉTRO-VAL

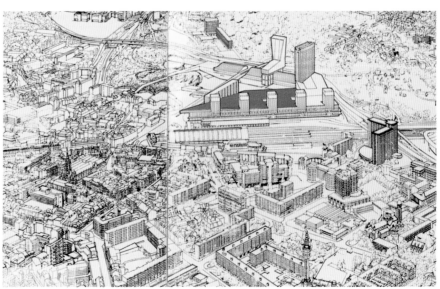

Index

Shopping centers are introduced in alphabetical order. Since their data denote those collected in November 1993, kindly understand subsequent changes, if any. Items covered are as follows:
<Graphic-sha editorial staff>

● Shop name · page
  1 : Address
  2 : Year in which shop opened
  3 : Developer
  4 : Design
  5 : Area
  6 : Number of cars parked
  7 : Key tenants
  8 : Number of tenants

アルファベット順に下記の要領にて収録しています。データは本書　取材時（1993年11月）のものです。変更されている場合もありますのでご了承ください。
グラフィック社編集部

● 店名·掲載ページ
  1 : 住所
  2 : 開店年
  3 : デベロッパー
  4 : 設計
  5 : 面積
  6 : 駐車台数
  7 : キーテナント
  8 : テナント数

5 : 30,100㎡
6 : 150
7 : Södermalms Saluhall
8 : 30

6 : 1,160

7 : Hennes & Mauritz, Intertoys, Van Piere Boeken, De Jong

8 : 115

1 : Kauppakeskus Itäkeskus TurunIlnnantie 4A SF-00130 Helsinki, Finland

2 : 1992

3 : Haka OY., Sponda OY.

4 : Juhani Pallasmaa, Heikkinen-Komonen OY., Helin & Siitonen,
    Hyvämäki-Karhunen-Parkkinen, Häkji & Karhunen

5 : 80,000㎡

6 : 2,500

7 : Anttila, Stockmann, CitySokos

8 : 170

1 : 122 Kings Road Chelsea London, SW3 UK

2 : 1988

3 : County and District Properties

4 : Crighton Mc Coll/Damond Lock Grabrowski

5 : 3,000㎡

6 : 0

7 : The Gap

8 : 22

1 : VerwaltungsgeslIschaft GmbH Kölnische Strasse 6 D-3500 Kassel, Germany

2 : 1991

3 : Brand Kasse(Kassel), Lebensversicherung AG(Nürnberger)

4 : Planbüro Dipl-Ing, M.Bode

5 : 10,000㎡

6 : 530

7 : Kaufhaus, Brinkmann, Möbenpic Hotel, Marché Restaurant

8 : 30

1 : 23 boulevard de la Madeleine 75001 Paris, France

2 : 1991

3 : Meiji Mutual Life Insurance Company(明治生命), Postel Investment Management Ltd.

4 : Jean Jacques Ory, Jean Michel Wilmotte

5 : 9,000㎡

6 : 0

7 : Madelios Monsieur, Madelios Madame, Silver Moon, Restaurant Les Trois Quartiers

8 : 70

1 : Place du Géneral de Gaulle 59000 Lille, France

2 : 1992

3 : SCI Lille Grand' Place, ARC Union, Espace Promotion

4 : Pierre Louis Carnèr

5 : 2,500㎡

6 : 0

7 : FNAC

8 : 14

ガレリア
ヨーロッパのショッピングセンター26

1994年10月25日　初版第1刷発行

著者	武藤聖一
発行者	久世利郎
印刷・製本	凸版印刷(新嘉坡)私人有限公司
写植	有限会社福島写植
英文	株式会社海広社
協力	
レイアウト	ぱとおく社
カバーデザイン	ウィークエンド株式会社
発行所	株式会社グラフィック社
	〒102 東京都千代田区九段北1-9-12
	電話03-3263-4318
	振替・00130-6-114345

ISBN4-7661-0792-6 C2052